2

Agriculture and the Common Market

AGRICULTURE
AND THE
COMMON MARKET

STANLEY ANDREWS

The Iowa State University Press, Ames

1 9 7 3

STANLEY ANDREWS, international consultant in agricultural development, is author of one other book and numerous articles on agriculture and international trade as well as reports on surveys in more than thirty countries. He was involved in responsible positions in military government during and after World War II in Italy, West Germany, and Japan. For the past twenty years he has been active in many goverment agencies and programs relating to agriculture and has headed many U.S. delegations to the Food and Agricultural Organization of the United Nations as well as international councils on wheat, cotton, sugar, and rice. Now retired on a small citrus farm in the Rio Grande Valley in Texas, he continues an extensive program of writing and carrying out international assignments for the United States Department of Agriculture and the State Department and for private organizations.

© 1973 The Iowa State University Press, Ames, Iowa 50010
All rights reserved

Composed and printed by The Iowa State University Press

First edition, 1973

Library of Congress Cataloging in Publication Data

Andrews, Stanley, 1894–
    Agriculture and the Common Market.
    Bibliography: p.
    1. Agriculture—Economic aspects—European Economic Community countries. 2. European Economic Community. 3. Produce trade. I. Title.
HD1920.5.A64   382′.41   72–5374
ISBN 0–8138–0030–7

CONTENTS

ACKNOWLEDGEMENTS

THIS WRITER is indebted to Mr. D. O. Andreas, President of the Andreas Foundation of Minneapolis, Minnesota, and to Mr. D. W. Brooks, now retired chairman of the Georgia Cotton Producers Association of Atlanta, Georgia, for the financial support which made possible two major surveys—Eastern Europe in 1967 and Western Europe in 1968—which developed much of the original material used in this book. These personal observations of people and programs in action in the field of agriculture in these two sections of Europe were invaluable in developing a perspective and an understanding of the Common Market and its implications for international agricultural trade.

I am indebted to many individuals in six countries in Eastern Europe and eleven countries of Western Europe and the Mediterranean, as well as the United States, who gave freely of their time and knowledge. Among the more than 100 persons interviewed were international bankers, government officials, farm leaders, cooperative marketing groups, international traders, and the usually anonymous individuals in many institutions and agencies who develop the material upon which decisions are made. The staffs of the Economic Research Service and the Foreign Agriculture Service of the United States Department of Agriculture were especially helpful. The staffs of such international institutions as the Economic Commission for Europe, the General Agreement on Tariffs and Trade, the European Office of the Food and Agriculture Organization of the United Nations, and the information offices of the European Community and the European Free Trade

Association all had their share in supplying data upon which some of the judgments and projections in this book are made.

Literally dozens of persons deserve recognition in the preparation of the manuscript. I especially want to thank Dr. Oscar Zaglitz, for many years a member of the staff of U.S. Missions in Brussels and Geneva and intimately concerned with agricultural developments in the Common Market, for his assistance in defining the scope of this effort and for guidance on the technical phases of Common Market operations. Dr. Richard E. McKenzie, fellow at the Harry S. Truman Library Institute, read the manuscript; his editorial assistance was invaluable in the final preparation. Mrs. Lois B. Koptezke typed the original taped notes on the European surveys and typed and retyped the original manuscript through several revisions and additions. Mrs. Laura Heller of the Harry S. Truman Library typed the final version. To both of these ladies who worked through scribbles and crossed-out words, caught errors, and came up with a readable manuscript, my sincere thanks.

For all of those who helped, named and unnamed, my hope is that the final product is worthy of their generous assistance and support.

STANLEY ANDREWS

INTRODUCTION

WITH SO MUCH SAID and written about the Common Market, why write more? Especially why single out agriculture as a special subject? Why is agriculture in the Common Market of major interest to the United States, and why have agricultural problems become a major concern of U.S. foreign policy? These are questions the casual reader may well ask. I do not attempt to give all the answers; I can only hope to high-light some of the questions, put the issues into some sort of perspective, and explore some of their implications for American agriculture and international agricultural trade.

The creation of a common economic grouping of six European states was a major development of this century. The agreements in 1971 to enlarge the Common Market by admission of Great Britain, Den-mark, Ireland, and Norway will create a trade area of 300 million people with a gross national product second only to the United States. The volume of annual external trade is more than $50 billion. This sum is only slightly less than the combined external trade of the United States and Russia. Agriculturally the area has been in the past—and still is in some categories—a major importer of products of American farms. Rapid agricultural development within the original Common Market Six since 1962 has resulted in major surpluses in many products and a self-sufficiency of about 92 percent; oilseeds, feed grains, beef, and veal are the primary deficiencies. The United Kingdom has been the world's largest importer of agricultural products. Denmark and Ireland are surplus producers of major temperate zone products. The addition of these four nations to the original Six will drop the self-sufficiency to about 85 percent. For a time the area as a unit will be a major importer of most of the traditional products which the United Kingdom has purchased from abroad. However, the acceptance by the United Kingdom and its three partners of the Common Agricultural Policy (CAP) means that as surpluses pile up, Great Britain's traditional supplies will come from within the area rather than from outside.

Agriculture is a special subject of concern because of its central role in the formation of the Common Market. The very existence of the Common Market in several instances hinged on successful compromises or agreements on agricultural problems. The Kennedy Round of General Agreement on Tariffs and Trade (GATT) negotiations in 1967 was stalled and on several occasions near breakup until last-minute agreement among the Six and the Contracting Parties on the agricultural issue.

In final negotiations for the admission of the United Kingdom the biggest hurdle (with the possible exception of Britain's portion of the Commission budget) was that of agriculture: What to do about the dairy products of tiny New Zealand and protection for Commonwealth sugar producers?

The United States, one of the principal outside supporters of the Common Market idea, finds itself torn between the ideal of freer international trade (as exemplified by the Reciprocal Trade Agreement Act of 1934) and the growing pressure for greater protection (as called for by some seventy industries and certain segments of agriculture itself) in legislation before Congress in 1971–72. The protectionist policies adopted by the Common Market are threatening some of the lucrative American agricultural exports to Europe. At the same time, by dumping certain surpluses in third-country markets, the Community adversely affects U.S. agricultural trade. If a trade war should develop, U.S. agriculture would probably suffer more than U.S. industry.

Although agriculture, in the view of most authorities, made the Common Market functional, it remained one of the basic problems to be faced as the Common Market entered the decade of the 1970s. Unquestionably, much has been accomplished in the integration of agriculture within the Common Market. When the CAP began to take shape following the Treaty of Rome in 1957, the six countries— France, Belgium, Luxembourg, Italy, the Federal Republic of West Germany, and the Netherlands—were faced with reconciling some 30,000 different rules and regulations affecting agriculture. Without this reconciliation no amount of industrial tariff reduction or barrier elimination would have made sense. The necessity to face up to this situation and the persistence of the leaders of the Common Market brought about the CAP, which to date is about the only really common approach to any internal segment of the Common Market. A common external tariff was established in 1967. In the works now are moves toward a common transportation policy, labor laws, corporate law revision, common sanitary regulations, and other stickier problems including the establishment of a common currency by 1980.

It was agriculture that saved the Common Market from dissolution. The vote of the French farmers in the 1965 French elections deterred General de Gaulle from scuttling the Common Market. Thus the European Economic Community—now officially the European Community (EC)—is a fact of life. The admission of the United Kingdom and three of her European Free Trade Association (EFTA) partners means that the United States will be faced with some difficult and perhaps far-reaching decisions in the decade ahead.

The liberalized trade policy of the United States has paid off handsomely during the past thirty-eight years. Whether this liberal policy can be continued with the present pressure for protectionism and the sometimes harshly protective stance of the Common Market is the big question. Statistics well illustrate changes that have occurred since the United States adopted a policy of freer international trade. Total world trade during the 1932–33 trade year was exceedingly low, and U.S. exports were among the lowest of the major trading nations: total exports of $1.4 billion with agricultural exports only $590 million. By 1953 world trade was beginning to recover from the abnormal conditions of World War II and the postwar food crisis. In that year total world trade amounted to $78 billion; U.S. agricultural exports totaled $2.3 billion. In the 1955–56 trade year U.S. agricultural exports totaled $3.5 billion. However, solid dollar exports (non-P.L. 480 and semicommercial trade) were $2.1 billion. Of this total figure the countries of the European Community purchased goods worth $1,644 million—considerably more than half the total commercial agricultural exports. By the trade year 1965–66 U.S. commercial exports to all countries had more than doubled, running to $5,113 million. Semicommercial exports and those under P.L. 480 brought the total to $6,681 million. Of this the European Community again took slightly more than $1,600 million worth of U.S. agricultural products. The list ran from $1.5 million worth of dairy products to $433 million in rice and other grains, $208 million for soybeans, more than $151 million for cotton, and $32 million for tallow.[1]

Aside from the pure economics of international agricultural trade policy (which are bound to be affected as the groupings of European states become larger), the problem of supplying the world with food and alleviating hunger must be dealt with. There is clamor that the world will face food shortages and possible mass starvation in the decades ahead unless we devise better balance between the growing world population and food production. In most of the Asian countries—Thailand, Ceylon, Burma, and the Mekong basin of Indo-China excepted—vast numbers of people are already undernourished if not

1. Dr. Oscar Zaglitz, Agricultural Trade and Trade Policy, report of National Advisory Commission on Food and Fibre.

near starvation. The same condition exists in some parts of South America and Africa. On the other hand, the problem of the industrialized countries of the Western World is to find means by which farmers may dispose of their abundance profitably. Most authorities argue that the current problem is more a matter of improving poor nutrition rather than preventing starvation. More extensive application of known technology in agriculture and better distribution of existing supplies are the primary problems of the 1970s.

Thus agriculture and the people who produce the food of the world have become very important in world politics. The ambassador who cannot talk in terms of food nutrients, diet levels, conversion ratios, gate prices, intervention levies, and support prices, or who does not have someone on his staff who can deal with these terms meaningfully, is not in the center of things. Food and the world food problem occupy the time of the modern statesman second only to peace and war.

The United States has traditionally depended on Europe to absorb most of our surplus agricultural production. For about the first 150 years the products of our farms were used to meet the interest and foreign exchange requirements for our purchases of industrial goods and capital funds from Europe. At the end of World War I we changed from a debtor to a creditor nation; although our foodstuffs, fibers, and animal industrial products were in demand, we had no certainty Europe would take them at the same prices. Between the wars, rising production in Europe; increasing competition from Latin American, African, and Eastern European countries; and our own massive efforts to maintain better prices for domestic producers caused American exports to decline, although they were still of major importance. With the end of World War II it was American agricultural production, along with that in our sister country Canada, that kept Europe from starvation. In the postwar period the United States regained much of its early role as supplier of European food and fiber and even added two major crops, grain sorghums and soybeans, which hardly existed as export items in the United States prior to World War II. The heady atmosphere of a profitable agricultural trade following World War II and pride in the technological explosion in American agriculture in the past twenty-five years blinded us to what was happening in our own country as well as Europe.

The traditional family farm—mainstay of American agriculture during the past century—has been disappearing at the rate of about 100,000 farms per year for the past twelve years. In this age of specialization it seems to be on the way out as an economic unit. While economists and agricultural authorities disagree on the details, there is some realization that the mere application of new technology and specialization-for-efficiency-at-all-costs do not solve the farm problem except for the very few. The social costs of the dislocation of millions of persons, even though their incomes were measurably less while they remained in agriculture, has perhaps been greater than if some far-reaching program had been devised to help them remain in rural areas. Western Europe, long committed to keeping a high portion of its people on the land, has gone to great lengths to raise the living standards of peasant agriculture. However, in attempts to make maximum use of modern machinery, the European Community is seeking over the long term to reduce the number of persons fully engaged in agriculture; to consolidate the small farms into larger tracts; and to provide greater health, education, and vocational training facilities for those who do not leave rural areas. One of the excuses for the Community's highly protective stance on agricultural products is that it seeks to maintain a higher standard of living for those engaged in farming and to avoid the situation that has transpired in the United States which Europeans believe has been caused by unplanned and too rapid application of modern technology.

In a previous time—in fact for a century and a half—the migration from rural areas to the cities greatly strengthened the American economy. The surplus youth from the farms manned the factories and the industries of the future. Since World War II this movement to the cities has been less than a blessing. To stop the trend, let alone reverse it, will require massive reinvestment in rural America. Here in the most affluent country in the world, with the most efficient farmers in the world, we find that 40 percent of the people with incomes below the official poverty level live in rural America. The quality of life reflected in rural housing, communications, education, health, and other public services is probably far below that which a household dweller in modern America has some right to expect.

Europe is unwilling to correct its farm problem by dumping the excess of farmers into the cities. We in the United States will sooner or later have to face up to the consequences of unlimited movement to urban areas and will have to decide on a desirable level of total population in agriculture. As these issues receive more attention on both sides of the Atlantic in this decade, the United States will face some alternatives which may well determine the character of rural America for the next quarter-century.

Agriculture and the Common Market

Chapter 1

ORIGIN AND STRUCTURE OF THE COMMON MARKET

IN 1957 six sovereign states of Western Europe created the European Community or Common Market, an act which has been hailed as the most significant economic and political development of the past century. The Treaty of Rome containing the terms of the agreement has been called by some knowledgeable observers one of the most important documents in Europe's history. Although the concept of economic and political integration was not new for Europe, apparently the political and economic climate in the years after World War II was just right for the statesmen of the period to develop a better system for peacetime cooperation.

In the numerous wars in the long history of Europe, one nation or another had tried to force a stronger military and economic grouping by taking over other states. As far back as 1834 five German states had seen the advantage of economic cooperation; they created a customs union which abolished tariffs between union members and established common custom duties. Between World War I and World War II political federation among the European states was much discussed. At that time statesmen sought to create stability through better economic and political groupings of the small states that came into being with the breakup of German and Austrian empires. These efforts had both political and economic overtones. A more unified Europe would strengthen the continent economically against American and Soviet economic growth and British power. During the 1920s and early 1930s proposals for various kinds of unification were advanced by committees of the League of Nations, the International Chamber of Commerce, and other groups. In 1921 Luxembourg and Belgium worked out a customs union. In May 1930 Aristide Briand, French Prime Minister, issued his famous memorandum proposing the "organization of the Regime of Federal Union." In 1931 Edouard Herriot's book, *The United States of Europe,* reflecting proposals currently in vogue at the time, called for a loose federation of European states and subsequent integration and unification by sectors of the economy through the device of international cartels. A series of industrial agreements, Herriot said, would stabilize production and employment, rationalize production, and lower costs. He argued that the business community in the United States had promoted federation in order to create more uniform and stable business conditions and that Europe should follow this early American example.

FOOD PROBLEM

Ironically, in all these discussions at the League of Nations and in most of the chancelleries of Europe, not a word was spoken about the necessity of rationalizing or coordinating European food production. The only international development relating to agriculture during this period of change and ferment was the creation of the International Institute of Agriculture in Rome, and that was largely promoted and brought into being through the efforts of an American agricultural attaché. The rise of Fascism in Italy and the later German financial crisis plus the rise of Hitler banished all ideas of European unification until the end of World War II.

In the months after the armistice starvation and political chaos threatened most of Europe. Winston Churchill viewed the scene grimly in the winter of 1946: "What is the plight to which Europe has been reduced? Over vast areas a quivering mass of tormented, hungry, care-worn and bewildered human beings gape at the ruins of their cities and homes, and scan the dark horizons for the approach of some new peril."

In that year President Harry Truman sent former President Herbert Hoover on a world tour to survey and report on the developing crisis in the world's food supply. The report of the Hoover Food Survey dramatized as nothing else could the fragmented, closed, and highly nationalistic production and distribution systems which had been the plague of Europe for centuries. Food shortages became acute during 1947 when millions in Europe faced starvation. Reserves in Europe were exhausted, and virtually the only places in the world where food stocks were above minimum needs of the local population were in the United States and Canada.

The United States was able to supply the additional 500 million bushels of grain needed to see Europe through the winter, but the crisis prompted a number of efforts to deal with the basic problem. At the lower levels of government—especially in the food and agriculture staffs of the occupation forces in Germany—attempts were made in informal conferences to break the traditions and bureaucratic log jams which restricted the free movement of food supplies, inputs, and production information across borders. Food conferences were held in Paris and London, where committees worked on plans that might enable Europe to feed itself better in the years ahead. Some committeemen talked of proposing a sort of "international commerce clause" which would permit tariff-free movement of any food product or input for food production between the states of Western Europe. The only developments coming out of these discussions were an improved system of dissemination of agricultural information to all countries and the establishment of training centers and international conferences which facilitated the flow of agricultural research between the countries. Some coordination in the use of research facilities enabled the best equipped stations to carry out the major research tasks regardless of the country in which the station was located. In addition, the old military research center at Volkenrode near Hanover, Germany, which had produced the buzz bombs that harassed London, was saved from destruction and turned into an agricultural and food research center.[1]

While discussions about food took place at lower levels, the statesmen of Europe—led by Konrad Adenauer of Germany, Premier Alcide DeGasperi of Italy, Foreign Minister Robert Schuman of France, and Paul Henri Spaak of Belgium—were concerning themselves with building a stronger Europe. Their major purpose was to counter the growing Communist strength in Eastern Europe; their major problem was to find some way to ease the tension between the two long-time enemies, France and Germany.

The statesmen of Europe had achieved little by 1948 when the United States entered the European economic and political picture with the Marshall Plan. In the four years following the creation of the Organization for European Economic Cooperation (OEEC), the decision-making body of the plan, sixteen countries received a $12 billion infusion of capital and goods. A time schedule was proposed for elimination of some of the restrictions on European trade and establishment of strong central committees to coordinate food production and export trade. The United States and some European leaders hoped that the cooperation brought about by OEEC would result in closer liaison on all political, economic, and military matters. Some—among them Chancellor Adenauer and DeGasperi—dared to hope that the cooperation might move to integration.

BEGINNING OF INTEGRATION

Jean Monnet—French diplomat, banker, planner, and one of the originators of U.S. wartime lend-lease—believed that a merger of the

---

1. This cooperation continues among some 16 European countries; so far as agricultural information and research are concerned, Europe is united.

coal and steel industries of Germany and France would be one means of easing tension between the two countries and at the same time make better use of the coal resources of the Ruhr and the iron mines of Alsace-Lorraine. Robert Schuman, French Foreign Minister in 1950, modified the idea and launched the Schuman Plan, embodying what became the European Coal and Steel Community (ECSC), as a first practical step toward European unification. France, the Republic of West Germany, Belgium, the Netherlands, Luxembourg, and Italy were the original members.

Formally established in 1952, the ECSC eliminated all restrictions among the six member states on exports, imports, and currency exchange which affected coal, scrap iron, and iron ore. Under the supernational powers provided in the treaty the first international tax, a levy on coal and steel production in member countries, took effect. Great Britain, an active member of the OEEC and a major steel and coal producer, gave her blessing to the effort but did not join the Six. Through the years Britain exchanged technical and trade information with the ECSC but declined formal association.[2] The institutions created to manage and govern the Coal and Steel Community established the pattern which was broadly followed later in the creation of the Common Market and Euratom (see Chapter 9). The institutional components established by ECSC are:

1. The High Authority which is the executive and law-making body and which acts by majority vote. It consists of nine independent members, each representing the community as a whole rather than his individual country. The High Authority is assisted by a large professional staff which administers the day-to-day work of the ECSC.

2. The Council of Ministers which represents the interests of the individual countries. In some cases the Council acts by a qualified majority but usually by unanimous decision. A consultative committee of fifty-one members representing workers, consumers, and dealers assists the Council in policy decisions and acts as an advisory body to the High Authority.

3. The Court of Justice which "ensures the rule of law in the application and interpretation of the Treaty." It is the supreme court of the ECSC and consists of seven judges appointed for six years by agreement among the governments of the six states. The decisions of the court are final and binding.

4. The Common Assembly or Parliament which consists of members appointed each year from the parliaments of the six governments. The treaty provided for election of members by popular vote, but thus far this provision has not been put into effect. The Parliament is required to meet once a year and may meet in extraordinary session

---

2. With the United Kingdom's admission to the Common Market in 1973 Britain will become a full member of the ECSC by 1978.

on its own initiative or that of the High Authority or the Council of Ministers. Its major function is to receive, review, and approve the annual report of the High Authority. It has no law-making power or power over the Council of Ministers, but it may, and frequently does, "give its opinion."

Many complex and difficult adjustments had to be made by each of the ECSC states which involved their transportation systems, energy supplies, external commercial policy, relocation of industries, and social affairs—all in the face of dire predictions of failure by opponents of the plan. The apparent success of the first three or four years convinced even the doubters that Europe would thrive even more with greater integration of its basic economies. Monnet and some others in OEEC fought for European union on a wider scale, but they failed to receive wide support from a majority of national leaders.

The United States, in its announcement of the Marshall Plan in 1947, had invited the countries of Eastern Europe and Russia to participate in the postwar rebuilding of Europe. The invitation was spurned by Russia, and Russian pressure kept at least two Eastern European states (Poland and Czechoslovakia) out of the association. With the increasing intensity of the cold war, the major thrust and concern of the OEEC became military. By 1949 the North Atlantic Treaty Organization (NATO) had been formed and had established the Western military posture against a Soviet-dominated monolith of Eastern Europe. Thus the cold war to a large extent dictated the overall political and economic developments in Europe and dominated U.S. policy for nearly two decades.

BIRTH OF THE COMMON MARKET

An attempt by OEEC, strongly urged on by the United States, to form a European Defense Community (EDC) floundered on a French veto. The EDC was to be a forerunner of what some hoped would be a European Political Community built around the OEEC countries. However, with failure of the EDC and the success of the ECSC, leaders of the Six were convinced that cooperation in other areas of their economies would work. A conference of the six ministers in Rome in 1957, presided over by Paul Henri Spaak of Belgium, drafted the Treaty of Rome, and the European Economic Community (Common Market) and Euratom were born. Its 278 articles and 378 complex pages in the English translation ushered in a new era for Europe.

The Rome Treaty is an impressive document. While many of its provisions are specific, the treaty is broad enough in scope to accommodate almost any amount of integration among the Six. The core of the treaty, however, is the formation of a customs union and the creation of common social and political institutions to serve this group of national sovereignties.

Among the specific objectives set out were:

1. Removal of customs duties and import and export quotas between each of the Six.

2. Establishment of a common tariff and commercial policy for states outside the Community.

3. Abolition within the Community of obstacles to the free movement of persons, services, and capital.

4. Inauguration of common agricultural and transport policies.

5. Establishment of a system insuring competition.

6. Adoption of procedures for coordination of domestic policies and for remedying balance of payments disequilibrium.

7. Removal of differences in national laws necessary for the operation of a common market.

8. Creation of a European social fund for education and training of displaced workers.

9. Establishment of a European investment bank to facilitate economic expansion.

10. Association of dependent overseas territories with the Community.

The Treaty also provided for institutions similar to those of the ECSC which would operate the European Economic Community and Euratom. The exception was that in place of the High Authority a commission composed of nine members would become the law-making and executive body. Two new management committees—the Economic and Social Committee (101 members) and the Consultative Committee (51 members)—would take the place of the consultative committee used in ECSC organizations.

In addition, nine specialized bodies advise on particular subjects: the Monetary Committee, the Short-Term Economic Policy Committee, the Medium-Term Economic Policy Committee, the Committee of Central Bank Governors, the Budgetary Policy Committee, the Transportation Committee, the Administrative Commission for Social Security for Migrant Workers, the Scientific and Technical Committee, and the Nuclear Research Consultative Committee.

Provision was made in the Rome Treaty for an amalgamation of the three executive bodies into one commission. This was not accomplished until 1967 when a single commission replaced the three separate bodies. By the end of the transition period on December 31, 1969, the two commissions and the High Authority had been completely amalgamated except for separate staffs which each maintained because of the particular problems of day-to-day operations in the vast system.

The Common Market idea captured worldwide attention. The

Eastern European response was the creation of Comecon, an economic community built around the Soviet Union. This did not develop into the rigid system visualized by the Soviet Union and anticipated by the West, especially by the United States. It was soon apparent that Czechoslovakia, Poland, Yugoslavia, Bulgaria, Hungary, and Romania—with centuries of traditional and economic ties to Western Europe—could hardly switch their orientation overnight to the East. Although trade in Eastern Europe over the last two decades has been largely dominated by the Soviet Union, the eastern nations are one by one, slowly and apparently with Russian assent, establishing economic arrangements with the West (see Chapter 13). The six principal Eastern European states allied with the Soviet Union are moving rather independently along broad economic rather than ideologic lines, even though they follow the foreign policy line of the Soviet Union. Even in matters of foreign policy there is not always a solid position on all issues. Romania and Yugoslavia have developed an independent course in foreign policy, with Czechoslovakia and Hungary moving toward greater independence in economic matters. For example, Romania has not supported the Communist line on the Israeli-Arab conflict and in 1968 signed a trade agreement whereby Israel sells considerable industrial goods to Romania in return for corn, wheat, and oilseeds. The Soviet invasion of Czechoslovakia in 1967 nipped the liberalization movement in that country; however, it did not stop but merely slowed down the efforts of Czechoslovakia to develop better trade relations with Western countries.

Acting under the mandate of the treaty to remove customs duties and import and export quotas, the Common Market in 1958 reduced tariffs on industrial goods by 50 percent between each of the Six and removed a large number of products from the quota list. The agricultural sector was given until December 31, 1961, to develop a common agricultural policy to eliminate barriers on agricultural products and to work toward a common tariff and trade policy with countries outside the Six.

AGRICULTURAL SECTOR

The agricultural sector has been one of the most difficult to bring to some sort of integration. The problem has been complicated by the fact that agriculture has entered into the center of the world political and economic stage. Once largely taken for granted, the European farmer or the peasant is no longer apart from the mainstream of world pressures and politics. Part of this new status for European agriculture has grown from the challenge which the Common Market posed for the free world outside the Market and the Communist bloc. Another reason has been the terrifying possibility that world population growth may soon outstrip ability to feed the people of this earth. (The disparity between those with food abundance and those who have too little is one of the perplexing problems facing farmers, world diplomats, and politicians.) Not only is there the age-old problem of hungry and starving people in remote corners of the world, but great segments of the rural population in nearly all countries are struggling to keep economic and social pace with the urban areas. Every government must be concerned with a rural problem, whether it is a lack of production to meet its food needs or too much production which bears down prices and squeezes more sharply the hard-pressed producer. Former colonial countries whose economies were developed largely to complement other investments of the ruling power find themselves with falling markets for their special cash crops and no solid base upon which to build a food program for their own peoples. Many of the economic difficulties and much of the political unrest in some of the developing countries of Africa and Asia grow out of their struggle to retain the markets and high prices for the specialized crops they once produced for the assured prices and markets of a colonial power. The problems of overabundance are just as complex and hard to handle as those of malnutrition.

The whole field of agriculture has been taken from the purely local or domestic sector and thrown into the international area of world economics, power politics, and diplomacy. International agreements on wheat, sugar, and coffee; commissions on cotton, wool, and many other commodities; United Nations trade development conferences; quota systems; tariff negotiations; import controls; and subsidies all have to be dealt with. What one nation does to support the income of its agricultural producers almost invariably affects producers or consumers of another country.

Many of the high aims and political objectives envisioned in the first years of the development of the Common Market have fallen by the wayside. It may require another quarter-century or another great upheaval in world relationships before the opportunity comes to create the Atlantic Community or a United Europe extending to the Carpathians. However, the Common Market as an economic entity is a fact of life. Political problems in Western Europe will continue to place great strains on unity, but the sheer economic values demonstrated in the past twelve years are such that no member of the Six can afford to break it up. This means that, unless there is a major shift of attitude, the European Community will continue to be highly protective in its outlook toward agricultural and industrial trade with nonmembers. Some of the protectionism, however, is bound to erode against the pressures and countermeasures of countries outside. It therefore appears that in the next ten years of the Common Market the members will struggle between maintaining the tightly knit economic unit which they now are—an island in a much larger world—and broadening the market into a true European community with all its economic and political connotations. Growing nationalism likely will prevent a federation with a central government; probably the present cooperation and broad political consultation will continue. In these developments of the future, agriculture will continue to be a key problem in achieving a truly free or reasonably liberal market policy between the Common Market—whatever its composition—and the outside world.

Chapter 2

AGRICULTURE AND THE TREATY OF ROME

TEN SECTIONS and nine articles in the Treaty of Rome dealing with agriculture give some indication of the importance which the drafters of that treaty attached to the agricultural sector of the six countries involved. Events in the twelve years since the signing of that document have amply illustrated both the vital role of agriculture in the economy of the Six and the difficulties of trying to reconcile divergent interests and the systems that each country had devised to protect its agricultural producers. It was naive to assume, as some did, that a few strokes of the pen and the announcement of a few general principles could wipe away the highly protective system built into the economic system of each country over the years. The agricultural sector could not be subjected overnight to the "discipline of international competition." The treaty makers knew their farmers and their countries and they understood the problem. Between the two world wars each member of the Six had devised elaborate and effective schemes to protect all or some segment of its agricultural economy from competition both from within and outside Europe. The depth and complexity of the problem were the main reasons the treaty makers gave the farm sector two years to come up with a workable plan to integrate agriculture.

Informal discussions of food problems in the postwar period revealed a diverse array of quotas, special freight rates, exchange restrictions, tariffs, border taxes, and packaging and sanitary regulations which hampered and often prevented the best use of available resources. In 1949 an eleven-nation food conference had been held in Bonn, Germany, to devise ways and means of increasing production and re-

12

ducing the drain of Europe on world food resources. The conference discussed and proposed a "Green Plan" which, among other things, argued for the prevention by law of the destruction of food for the purpose of creating a scarcity and high prices. This plan was written into the new West German Federal Constitution and was observed for a time by other countries of Europe. This declaration today is of some embarrassment to West Germany where occasionally the government finds that it would be advantageous to destroy food or artificially hold down production. The problem of better distribution of agricultural products throughout Europe had come up informally at an OEEC ministers' meeting in Rome in 1951. In 1952 at another OEEC meeting, France had suggested the "Green Meadow program" which, had it been put into effect, would have created an International Agricultural Institute for Economic Planning and Studies. The idea later became a reality in Switzerland as the Green Meadow Foundation, which functions as an International Center for Economic and Social Studies and holds meetings and annual seminars open to representatives of all Western European states. All these early moves merely foretold some of the problems which were ahead when implementation of the Treaty got under way.

Objectives for Agriculture

Five basic objectives of a common market for agriculture were listed in the ten sections and nine articles of the Treaty:

1. To increase overall agricultural productivity.
2. To insure a fair standard of living, particularly by increasing the individual earnings of persons engaged in agriculture.
3. To stabilize markets.
4. To guarantee regular and ample supplies of agricultural products.
5. To insure reasonable prices to consumers.

The writers of these objectives seemed to recognize the hard facts of agricultural life in nearly every country in the world—namely, a lack of balance between production and markets and a level of income among agrarians lower than that among the industrial segments of society. These conditions were especially evident in the Six where extensive measures were used by each country to protect agricultural producers from the competition of low-priced imports of certain agricultural products, to encourage production of others, and to increase the country's self-sufficiency. One cannot ignore the fact that the outcome of numerous wars and conflicts in Europe over the centuries has hinged more than once on an adequate food supply. No government in the modern world can long exist without some demonstration to its people that it can provide them with a minimum subsistence.

COMMON POLICY REQUIREMENTS

In the two years of study and negotiation by a special committee following the Treaty of Rome, the Council of Ministers developed a series of requirements which the Common Agricultural Policy (CAP) would have to meet.

1. Agriculture must be an integrated part of the economy as a whole and must be recognized as an essential factor in the life of society.
2. Improvement of agricultural structures must assure to capital and labor in European agriculture incomes compatible to those in other branches of the economy.
3. Production and forthcoming demand must be balanced with due consideration to imports and exports.

Stating the broad objectives and the guidelines to achieve them is relatively simple in the confines of a committee or commission board room; putting the bricks and boards into some sort of relationship to achieve those objectives and meet such requirements is definitely another matter.

Some persons in the United States tend to equate the problem of economic integration of the six European countries with that which faced the thirteen colonies in North America when our Constitution was adopted. The thirteen colonies had developed along different lines—industry, commerce, and fishing in New England; agriculture in the South. But that was in a time when industry was not so complex, when transportation was limited, when needs and wants were simpler, and when commerce consisted largely of supplying the few things a particular colony could not supply for itself. Europe—with centuries of commercial, political, and economic development behind it—was in 1957 the most industrialized area in the world. At the same time, land was a means of survival for millions of people; but by tradition land was fragmented by inheritance. Government intervention with practically every device known to the modern world was used at one time or another by the various countries to try to protect agriculture, producers, and the food and raw materials supply. The task of reconciling these built-in conflicts was cause for concern if not alarm. Sicco L. Mansholt, former minister of agriculture for the Netherlands and Vice-president of the Common Market Commission, pointed to the disparity between existing European conditions and the situation in the United States in a major address in 1960. At that time the Common Market countries contained 9 million individual farms, many of them in from five- to thirty-acre parcels. Of the 9 million farms, 5.5 million had less than twelve acres; total land in cultivation, including pastureland, was 40 million acres. This is in comparison to 400 million cultivated acres in the United States, or about 1/40th of our land resources.[1] Europe at the time employed 15 million agricultural workers—one worker for each 11 acres of land; the ratio in the United States at the time was one worker to 130 acres. Since 1960 a reduction in agricultural workers in Europe on a per acre basis has occurred, and in the United States the figure is now one worker for each 150 acres of land. The general ratio remains about the same, however.

Meeting the first requirement for a common agricultural policy—agriculture as an integrated part of the economy as a whole—meant bringing about revolutionary changes within as well as between each of the Six. Over the centuries Europe had developed great urban and commercial centers largely peopled by a highly educated middle and upper class. The royalty, merchants, and industrialists together with a highly skilled and tightly organized labor force enjoyed the educational facilities and health and social services of an advancing urban society. Generally speaking, the countryside remained in the hands of a peasant class with poor educational facilities, fewer of the amenities common in city life, and a decided lack of mobility between the rural and urban areas. In most European areas, in fact, it was policy to discourage movement because of the need to maintain a balance between rural and urban populations. European governments very early were anxious not to overcrowd the cities with people unskilled and unable to secure employment who would become clients on the relief rolls. There were many experiments, particularly in Germany, to develop a sort of bridge between the rural and the industrial areas. In most of the experiments the worker had his own small home and plot of land in the country and at the same time worked in the city. The idea was that by operating a small sundown farm, the family would have a home and a means of subsistence when work slowed down in the industrial areas. These efforts were rather widespread and reasonably successful in the period 1921–39. However, they were not on a scale large enough to materially affect the total picture.

In addition to the problems caused by long tradition, the Common Market came into being just about the time the technical revolution in agriculture hit Europe in the form of wide use of farm machinery and petroleum power. The degree of technical advance varied in each country and was reflected in the overall agricultural policies in each country.

The second requirement for a common agricultural policy—that of

---

1. This is a round figure usually used in describing land in cultivation and in pastures in the United States. All class 1 to 3 land regarded as arable totals 637 million acres; total land use for crops in 1965 totaled 336 million acres, of which 37 million was in fallow. Crops were harvested from 294 million acres in 1969.

structural change in agriculture—was even more difficult. It would have been politically (if not economically and physically) impossible to uproot the old intensive agriculture based primarily on small acreage, high hand labor input, and high production per acre and replace it with a system which gauged efficiency in terms of output per man rather than per acre. Labor shifted from the rural sector could not have been readily absorbed in the industrial areas. A situation similar to what has come about in the United States in the urban areas might well have developed. A change in the farming structure was recognized as a necessity, but over a long period of time. The administrators of the common policy would be required to protect the older structure through the period of change. At the same time, means would need to be devised to bring the benefits of rapid technological change to the rural sector in each country.

Finally, the requirement that "production demand should be balanced with due regard to imports and exports" implied a market policy or common trade policy. This meant that the matters of tariffs and export and import control would have to be vested in a single central authority rather than in the individual countries. This further meant that in future negotiations with countries outside, the Six would speak as a group rather than as individual countries. Since there was no uniformity on the application of tariffs, market regulations, or import or export policies—even between various parts of the individual countries let alone among the Six—the friends of the Common Market idea found another mountain to climb before the worthy objectives of the Rome Treaty and the requirements for a common agricultural policy could be made operative.

Tariff Reductions

In the four years following the initial actions of the Common Market in January 1958 which reduced industrial tariffs by 50 percent, there was a remarkable industrial growth. Whether this industrial growth was directly attributable to the reduction of tariffs or whether Europe was simply ready for a surge forward is still debated by the economists. The fact remains that the economic growth rate of the Six became greater than that of either the United States or Great Britain in the first years of the treaty operation. Employment, wage rates, and purchasing power set new records.

Agriculture was not included in this first round of tariff reductions. Final agreement on the intricate and difficult task of making uniform the pricing, protection, and management of agriculture did not come until the closing hours of the Kennedy Round of GATT negotiations in Geneva in June 1967, nearly ten years after the signing of the Treaty. Prior to this, however, certain basic agreements emerged in January

1962 which seemed to point the direction that the Common Agricultural Policy would take. Agreement was reached on these points:

1. Control of farm products would be through Common Marketing authorities.

2. Common prices and the abolition of trade barriers within the area would be established during the transition period which then was visualized for 1962 to 1970. Later this target date was set up to June 30, 1968.

3. Control of imports from outside countries would be through variable levies, fees, minimum prices, and in some instances quantity and quality regulations. The United States had fought strongly against variable levies in favor of a minimum fixed tariff.

4. Levy funds and other common funds would be used to finance market operations and subsidize exports.

5. Quality standards and regulations would be uniform.

6. Veterinary, sanitary, health, and plant regulations would be uniform.

Many crucial decisions had to be made in the following years on other matters. Among them were the matter of external tariffs to replace the six separate national tariffs and the establishment of common pricing policies and regulations. Resolution of these matters would enable the Six to better engage with other participants in GATT. The U.S. Trade Expansion Act was due to expire on June 30, 1967.

Chapter 3

The Common Agricultural Policy

FOR THE FIRST TIME in the history of economic arrangements between states in Europe, the Rome Treaty and the Council guidelines specifically provided that agriculture must be treated as an integrated part of the economy as a whole. Developing a Common Agricultural Policy according to the guidelines and principles agreed upon by the Council of Ministers in 1958 fell to a special agricultural commission, whose major task was the development of a unified price and trade system which could be put into effect by the end of the accelerated transition period, June 30, 1968. This involved transforming literally thousands (estimated at 30,000) of rules, regulations, tariff schedules, and other measures into a common structure without wrecking the agricultural sector of any of the partners. A senior member of the agricultural staff of one of the Common Market countries described the dilemma as "a choice between many roads to the goal of a unified agricultural economy in the Common Market—each of them difficult and full of sink holes." The Treaty under which the agricultural group worked was first of all a political instrument, and the commission was subject to all the compromises and pressures of national and private interests to which any economic arrangement between individuals or nations is subject. The Treaty was also a social document; it specifically set out as one of the objectives raising the living standards of the rural population in each of the six member countries. Finally, the Treaty command for a Common Agricultural Policy required common prices, uniform subsidies, agreements, unified standards, and a common approach—applied internally as well as externally—to all questions of production and trade.

18

Each of the countries within the Six had its own way of intervening in agriculture. Each had its own rules and reasons for following a particular system—some to keep internal prices high, some to keep them low on certain products for the benefit of the urban populations. The correlation of these interventions into an operating system was the task. The working groups considered three approaches to the problem: (1) to establish general ground rules for trade and competition between the Six, and then to permit each country to work out its arrangement with other members or the outside countries; (2) to coordinate and unify all the various systems of supporting producer income into one uniform system in which the producers of each country would have equal chance in the marketplace and would stand or fall on their own working efficiency; or (3) to create a special agency which would not only set up rules and regulations but fix prices and provide a marketing system, with all that the term implies, for various commodities. The last alternative would mean establishing common prices, common support levels, and a system for unrestricted movement of agricultural products within the Six. A common marketing system also implied a common tariff in trade with countries outside the Market. The third alternative was adopted.

Instruments of Control

In 1962 the first of a long succession of marketing bodies began to control and supervise agricultural trade in various commodities. Three control instruments were to be used: variable import levies, import quotas, and quality controls. Wheat, coarse grains, sugar, and dairy products would be controlled through variable import levies. In the twelve-year transition period other products such as pork, beef, poultry, and eggs have become subject to the variable levy system. Import quotas were imposed on items such as live cattle. Movement of fruits, vegetables, nuts, wine, olive oil, and similar items would be controlled by enforcing quality standards. In emergency situations intervention levies or special purchases in the internal market for destruction or disposal out of the local market would be used. The use of quality controls follows in some degree the market order system in the United States whereby standards are manipulated to hold lower-quality products off the market in order to maintain a stronger price for the product. The system as it finally went into operation effectively insulated the producers of the Common Market countries from outside competition (see further details in Chapter 9).

Basic to the success of any operation of the Common Agricultural Policy was determining a mutually acceptable price level for agricultural products. First priority had to be given to the search for a price formula on the items which affected the greatest number of people and were basic to the overall agricultural sector. Grain prices fell into this category since varied forms of cereals accounted for 50 percent or more of the diet of the population of the Six. Feed grains and supplements were the very base upon which much of the remainder of the farm economy rested—livestock, poultry, and dairy products in particular. So wheat became the basic cereal in the pricing discussions of the marketing organization, and feed grains (corn, sorghum, millet) and other products used mainly for livestock feeding were priced on a conversion ratio related to wheat.

The basic outline of the policy and pricing system was issued and approved by the Agricultural Commission in 1962. Two years passed before a firm price policy for the transition period was announced. The grain price policy and prices for pigs, poultry, and dairy products were announced in January 1964, along with a schedule stating when each commodity would come under control. As an example, prices on dairy products, beef, and veal would become effective April 1, 1964; rice would come under control on July 1, 1964; vegetable oil and similar products were not finalized until November 1966. This scheme, however, did not then mean that one set of rules and regulations governed all agricultural matters in the Six. This was mainly an agreement on prices and intracommunity adjustments. It was not until June 1967— almost ten years after the Treaty of Rome—that the ministers of agriculture of the six member countries made the decisions which gave practical effect to the earlier agreements of January 1962 and December 1964, actively establishing common prices for cereals and common markets for pork, eggs, poultry, and oilseeds. This act in 1967 meant that finally intracommunity trade would be open and free. Even then, it was not possible to provide absolute intracommunity movement on livestock due to the many and varied veterinary regulations in each country. Sanitary regulations, quality standards, quotas, minute package and technical regulations also had the effect of restricting trade. However, grain prices and trade policy caused the most concern and continued to be the most difficult issue to resolve, from the standpoint of both intracommunity trade and external or import-export trade.

PROBLEMS AND COMPROMISES

In putting the Common Market into operation, the ministers and the Council confronted a number of difficult situations which to some extent overshadowed agricultural issues and even the extreme divergencies within the six member states. First was the seeming incompatibility between France and Germany. Germany—with a vast, modern, and highly efficient industrial complex—wanted access to the French market for its industrial products. France—with the largest agricultural potential—wanted access, and almost exclusive access, to the German market for it agricultural products. While other lesser issues involved the four other member states in varying degrees, this issue between France and Germany caused the most concern. France, a low-cost producer with a potential of high production, could and did sell its grain products at relatively low prices. Germany, on the other hand, had traditionally protected the income of its primary producers through a high-price policy on agricultural products and objected to the potential flood of cheaper French grain into Germany. Unless the transition period were long and the price adjustments moderate to a point where her producers could adjust to the new situation, the Germans argued, the agricultural sector of the German economy would be destroyed. The agreement in principle that came out of the deliberation of the Council in 1964 was in effect a political compromise between Germany and France. Target grain prices would not generally be higher than the German price of roughly $2.92 per bushel (paid in 1962) nor lower than the French price of roughly $2.17 per bushel. The common price set for August of the 1964–65 market season was between these two extremes. In terms of dollars, the Council decided on $106.25 per ton for wheat other than durum, $91.25 for barley, and $90.63 for corn. However, these prices did not go into full effect until July 1967, and in the transition period many of the existing regulations, subsidies, and quota restrictions were either eliminated or reduced. Under this system the German, Italian, and Belgian grain farmers took a price cut of some 12 percent for their grains. The Netherlands, a low-cost grain producer and large importer of grain products for feeding livestock and poultry, was most seriously affected by the new price structure. Here the price of wheat was raised from $61.75 per ton to $104.83; durum wheat from $75.50 to $117.26; rye $57.75 to $93.75; barley $54.10 to $91.25; corn $59.70 to $93.72. German, Italian, and Belgian consumers received a windfall reduction in food costs of about 13 percent as a result of the conversion ratios. All of these prices have since moved upward under the variable levy system.

The basic approach to the management of agriculture in the Common Market as provided for in the Common Agricultural Policy of 1962 has stood the test of practical operation, at least in the European view. The levy system in place of fixed tariffs for grains, beef, pork, poultry, and dairy products, while obnoxious in the American view, has worked for the six member states. The system of holding up farm income through price supports and facilitating exports through subsidies can hardly be criticized by American interests since it is the same system used to support agriculture in the United States. Intervention levies, which become effective when the actual price falls to a certain percentage below the target price, is another version of the countervailing duty system used by the United States to protect its agricultural and industrial interests from undue competition from outside. The third operative device, that of controlling the supply by manipulation of the quality standards, remained the standard method of control for fruits and vegetables. It should be noted, however, that the original directives had to be revised to allow more drastic methods to cope with wide price fluctuations of these products in the market. Between 1962 and 1964 changes were made to permit compensatory taxes or countervailing duties to become effective if prices within the market or in a given country fell below the so-called reference price. The reference price is calculated on the basis of the mean arithmetic price of farm prices during the preceding three years in member states, adjusted seasonably and for abnormal conditions. As in the grain price structure, if the actual price falls below the target or reference price by a given percentage, the government stands ready to buy all grain and other products offered.

The policy of assessing a levy on imports in order to maintain the target prices on grains within the market and of subsidizing exports with funds acquired through the levy system and through assessments on member states is running into some difficulties. The amount of subsidies needed to make export products competitive in the world market alarms the finance ministers. Presently the levies collected on imports do not yield the sums needed for the export subsidy. Each member state is therefore assessed for a proportionate share of the deficit in the Guarantee Fund which is used in the management of these products. (This was a major issue in the admission of Great Britain to the Market.) This problem is growing more serious as the six-country area becomes more nearly self-sufficient in the major agricultural products and imports fewer products on which it draws levies. The Market countries are now 92 percent self-sufficient outside of fiber crops, and those are duty free in most cases. Already the Six produce a surplus in soft wheat, sugar, and pork, and there are literally mountains of butter, poultry, and fruit and vegetable products.

Basic Assumptions

The basic assumptions on which the Common Agricultural Policy was projected were:

1. That the Common Market or any other grouping of Western European countries would be, for an indefinite future, a deficit area in basic agricultural products.

2. That the import levies provided for in the Common Agricultural Policy would provide the necessary funds to subsidize the exports of the few products which occasionally become surplus and, in addition, support the Guarantee and Guidance Fund to the extent needed for structural changes required to modernize European farming.

3. That the abolition of internal tariffs and other restrictions would bring about a high degree of specialization in agricultural production—that is, each country would produce for the total Market

those products which it could most efficiently produce and buy other products from efficient producers.

None of these assumptions has proved completely valid. The flexible levy system and other protective provisions of the Common Agricultural Policy have given European farmers incentives and, more importantly, the cash to modernize. The farmers in the Common Market have mechanized and become more efficient producers, but production patterns have remained about the same. Thus each country is merely producing more of its traditional crops. This has resulted in surpluses of nearly everything except feed grains and oilseeds and consequently less dependency on outside sources.

The variable import levies have been climbing higher each year, and more commodities are coming under the control system. Still, the levies do not produce the necessary revenue to subsidize export of surpluses of butter, poultry, pork, soft wheat, and other products which the Six are pouring into outside markets. The cost of subsidizing these exports is now approaching $3 billion annually. This subsidy program has been subject to continuous and agonizing review and was one of the issues which the Six settled in December 1969 (see Chapter 16). Finally, for a number of reasons, the hope of the planners for specialization in each country on main economic crops has not taken place. As an illustration of the problem, Germany does not fill all of its soft wheat requirements in France because German interests in Eastern Europe dictate that trade be reestablished with that area. Perhaps if quality were the single test, wheat from the United States would be more desirable in Germany. Social conditions in France and Italy offer other illustrations of the resistance to specialization. The small farmers of southern France resent the heavy importation of low-cost, high-quality poultry from the Netherlands; the French government has found it necessary for political reasons to undertake special measures to keep these small farmers in business. Structural adjustment in Italy is taking place slowly because Italy fears crowding with unskilled peasants her already overcrowded cities. Most experts agree that in time some specialization will come in some areas, but the process will be slow. In the meantime the Agricultural Commission and Council are wrestling with the problem of how to balance the undeniable benefits of specialization with the goal of equalizing income, living standards, and opportunity of the rural sector.

PRICE MAINTENANCE

In the view of the men in the Common Market headquarters at Brussels who are responsible for developing the techniques and procedures in the management of the agricultural sector, three methods might be used to maintain the present high prices on farm products within the Six and at the same time reduce the subsidy drain on the member states.

1. Production control.
2. World market regulation through international agreements similar to those now in effect for wheat, coffee, and sugar.
3. Improved structures in European agriculture—larger farms, fewer people in agriculture, more extensive use of machinery and modern technology, thus lowering prices but improving income for those still engaged in agriculture.

The first alternative, according to those responsible for policy in the Market, would be a poor choice psychologically in light of the present world food situation. The second—worldwide market regulations on wheat, olive oil, sugar, and eventually on feed grains, oil seeds, and rice—would be a major step. The third alternative will take time and a great deal of money, since it involves a basic change in the agricultural structure and a reduction in the number of persons depending on agriculture in each of the countries (see Chapter 16). This will be difficult to achieve without creating an imbalance between the urban and rural sectors. It will be politically difficult since at least 20 percent of the voters in the areas are either agriculturally based or influenced by what happens in agriculture.

Despite all the delays and near failures in achieving a workable arrangement for agriculture in the Six, an arrangement does exist. One observer at headquarters of the Common Market in Brussels has said that "an agreement is something, even though it may be a bad one. So long as there is working together as the present system requires, there is always opportunity and, indeed, probability of improvements. If no agreement existed we would be back where we started ten years ago." (2, 24)

Chapter 4

UNITED STATES AND THE COMMON MARKET

THE ECONOMIC STAKES are high for the United States in the Common Market. The political stakes are equally high. Since World War II we have pressed for greater political cooperation and unity among Western European states. Our thirty-eight-year-old policy of freer international trade, lower tariffs, and fewer barriers is under severe pressure and may be reversed as a result of developments in the Common Market which the influence of the United States helped to create.

Since the signing of the Rome Treaty in 1957–58, roughly 45 percent of our total export trade has been with the six countries of the European Community (EC). Nearly two-thirds of this has been in the products of American farms. Some of this agricultural trade has merely followed the traditional pattern of prewar years, except in a greater volume. The United States had formerly supplied cotton, wheat, tobacco, some feed grain, lard, apples, hides, sausage casings, pig livers, and a host of small items. Other exports to the Community (grain sorghums, soybeans—big items on today's list) hardly existed prior to World War II. Before 1941 soybeans mainly from China were an import item in the United States. Grain sorghums were almost all used domestically. Rice went largely to Cuba but now is an important item to Western Europe. Cotton, largest prewar export crop to the Continent and to members of the Six, has dwindled to a minor item.

AGRICULTURAL EXPORTS

In terms of total international trade, our agricultural exports between 1964 and 1969 have contributed an average of $1 billion per year in the U.S. balance of payments, a high percentage of which comes from the Common Market area. American farmers must depend on foreign sales of farm products to dispose of the yield of one of every five acres in cultivation. Farm exports in 1969 accounted for the crops grown on 58 million of the 294 million acres of harvested crops. Some 15 percent of the total farm output leaves the country compared to 8 percent for industry. At the time of the signing of the Rome Treaty, the Common Market absorbed 51 percent of our poultry exports, 36 percent of our soybeans, 36 percent of our feed grains, and 27 percent of our cotton. The highest point in U.S. agricultural exports to the Common Market prior to the record sales in 1970–71 came in the 1965–66 market year. Exports have leveled off since then and have been holding just over $1.3 billion, with an average overall for the ten-year period of around $1.4 billion. The latest figures (Table 4.1) indicate a change in the character of our exports to the Common Market—large increases in soybeans and a decline in the traditional exports of cotton, lard, and bread grains.

TABLE 4.1
U.S. AGRICULTURAL EXPORTS TO THE COMMON MARKET, 1961–70

	1961–62	1965–66	1968–69	1969–70
	($ million)			
Grains and rice, including wheat	433.9	708	382	327
Soybeans, cake and meal	208.3	428	437	559
Fruits, vegetables, and preparations	80	99.2	70	93
Tobacco	104.5	105	147	135
Tallow	32.3	36.3	17	21
Hides and skins	22	31.2	23	22
Poultry and eggs	66.7	31.8	15	14
Variety meats	16.7	33	32	41
Cotton	151.7	53.7	30	18
Corn by-products	0	0	34	33
Other commercial exports	63.8	111	112	119
Dairy products	1.6	18.5	1	1
Total	1,181.5	1,655.7	1,300	1,383

The dollar volume, as shown in Table 4.1, has averaged about $1.4 billion annually, with the highest point in 1965–66. The high dollar volume items have been changed. With the exception of cotton, the list of declining items almost parallels the list of products subject to variable levies. The major increases have been in the nonlevy, nontariff items bound by the General Agreement on Tariffs and Trades (GATT). Of the $356 million worth of variable levy products exported in 1969, corn represented $239 million, other feed grains $8 million, rice $32 million, wheat $47 million, and poultry and eggs $12 million. The dollar total for the nonvariable levy items was $1,028 million, with soybeans and tobacco showing the largest gains. It is plain that as an agricultural item comes under the Common Market management system, the variable levies go up and the volume goes down.

The volume of U.S. agricultural trade with the Common Market is still high, the largest dollar volume to any area in the world and equal to the combined exports to the United Kingdom and Japan. What happens in this decade in terms of the enlarged Common Market decisions to subject further products to the levy system is of vital and worldwide concern. These decisions will affect not only the economics of agricultural exports but also the overall trade policy and international relations of the United States.

INDUSTRIAL EXPORTS

Many of America's largest and most important industrial firms, once highly protective in their attitude, are now strongly supporting even freer and more open trade between the United States and Europe, particularly with the EC. This stems partly from the fundamental belief that only through freer trade can the economies of the world expand and develop. More important is the fact that many large American firms have built plants inside the EC area, purchased existing plants, merged or concluded patent arrangements with European firms, and find themselves behind the EC tariff wall. The United States is somewhat limited in its response by the struggle between forces desiring to lift trade restrictions further and those seeking to provide protection and relief for industries and farm products drastically affected by imports. Since all tariffs are abolished between the Six, some industries in each country are affected to some degree by competition from one or more of the countries within the Six. The external tariffs and the variable levy system very effectively protect the EC as a unit, but strictures within it from time to time result in special taxes, quotas, institution of sanitary regulations, and other restrictive devices. These are even more effective than a tariff in thwarting more liberalized trade. The statesmen, rank-and-file individuals, and industries of the world face the challenge of somehow reconciling the absolute necessity for increasing trade with the harsh adjustments which freer trade is bound to bring in some areas. While the United States is less restrictive in its current policies than some European countries, the fact that the most powerful nation in the world from time to time does invoke legal or voluntary restrictions against imports puts us in a poor position to insist too strongly that others reduce trade restrictions.

HISTORY OF U.S. TARIFFS

In an earlier period of U.S. history, when the United States had to buy industrial products from abroad and sold agricultural products in the world markets to pay for them, the problem was simpler. We enacted tariffs to protect our struggling new industries. We sold our abundant agricultural products and imported the industrial technology and goods to make our system work. Now we have the capacity to produce, in almost every category of agriculture and industry, far beyond any possibility of absorbing these products at home. We want to trade and trade big, sometimes forgetting that other countries have farmers who are also able to produce a surplus and industries which can expand beyond local needs. From the very beginning of our nation, the question of trade and protection of the home market has been a major political and economic issue. The question of whether tariffs should be for revenue only or for protection came up in the very first Congress in 1789 and was the concern of every administration for nearly 150 years. For one reason or another, tariff protection was usually on the high side until the administration of Woodrow Wilson, when the Underwood tariff became effective in October 1913. This was the first major and consistent reduction in tariffs in the history of the Republic. Still, the reduction was modest. The free list was increased and rates were reduced on 958 items, left unchanged on 307, and increased on fewer than 100. The average reduction was 26 percent. Unfortunately, the rates were never tested through long operation. Shortly, the United States joined the Allies against Germany and tooled up for World War I. Expensive plants were built, prices were high, and production boomed. At the end of the war both industry and agriculture sent out cries for protection against imports. A hastily drawn law in 1921 sought to soothe the discontent of farmers who were in the depths of a depression brought on by collapsing farm prices and overproduction. This was followed by the Fordney-McCumber tariff which established rates at the highest level in history. It also established the principle which gave the President the power to insure protection against imports by adjusting rates by 50 percent upward or downward. The Hawley-Smoot tariff of June 1930 set another record for high protection. Many of the leading economists of the time urged President Hoover to veto the bill. He declined, and the new law set off a wave of retaliatory legislation all over the world. For this and perhaps other reasons, trade began a disastrous decline. The U.S. depression (which the new tariffs were supposed to help cure) grew worse, war debt payments from Europe ceased, and from a combination of many circumstances the world economy seemed to grind to a standstill.

Cordell Hull, then a senator from Tennessee, was one of the few men in Congress at the time who argued against restrictive tariffs, believing that freer trade offered a way out of the depression. Hull became Secretary of State under President Roosevelt and in 1934 was the guiding force behind the Reciprocal Trade Agreements Act. Under this act a series of executive agreements with several countries made trade freer for the United States, and, through the most-favored-nation principle, trade was liberalized for other nations as well. Food shortages and low buying power after World War II, together with the rising threat of communism in Europe, brought a new approach by the United States to the trade problem. For the first time tariff trade policy involved more than domestic considerations. Foreign considerations became the basis for tariff-making, and the Secretary of State replaced the Secretary of the Treasury as the dominant influence in tariff negotiations. The liberalization proposed by Secretary Hull prior to World War II culminated, nearly fifteen years later, in the establishment in 1948 of the General Agreement on Tariffs and Trade (GATT). This agreement brought into being a formal international body devoted primarily to the reduction of trade barriers in international commerce, providing the framework for multilateral treaties. The United States, as a member of that body, is still directed largely by the principles in the Reciprocal Trade Agreements Act of 1934 by a system of bilateral agreements in which Congress remains the directive power but the President retains power to raise or lower tariffs within limits set by Congress.

While the principle of the Reciprocal Trade Agreements remains, additional powers were given the President in the Trade Expansion Act of 1962 which, among other things, also provided for the Kennedy Round of tariff negotiations. Under the 1962 law the President may make mutual trades and concessions on tariff rates with other nations; he may withdraw concessions on an individual country or area basis and deal with blocs of nations as a unit, especially the Common Market. Even broader powers were suggested for the President in the Trade Act of 1970 (see Chapter 17).

REACTIONS OF U.S. AGRICULTURE

From the end of World War II to the present, U.S. policy has supported the idea of the Common Market and of expanded world trade, with an attendant reduction of trade barriers. American farmers have generally supported the recent trade policy, and many of them no doubt are aware of the historic fact that foreign markets have absorbed our surpluses every year since the beginning of the United States. They have noted that international as well as domestic agricultural trade has become more and more controlled by government, and they have usually approved the formation of larger and more liberalized trading groups in Europe which might begin to break down some of the restrictions on tariffs, currency regulation, sanitary laws, taxes, and quotas. They have been disappointed. More than 90 percent of all agricultural commerce moves today under some restriction. In the past twelve years, American farmers have watched with concern and even dismay the multitude of problems and critical issues brought forward by the launching of the Common Market.

Many of the policies, rules, and regulations emerging from the

Common Market are directly contrary to the principles perceived by
the U.S. government on how the system should work. Early in 1962
Secretary of Agriculture Orville Freeman delivered a major address
before the ministerial meeting of the agriculture committee of the
Organization for Economic Cooperation and Development (OECD) in
Paris in which he outlined the U.S. government view on trade problems and policies. He set forth three basic principles and warned that
the United States would not look with favor on unlimited use of nontariff controls which might affect international trade. The U.S. position was that:

1. As provided in the OECD convention, trading arrangements
should be global and nondiscriminatory in character. Existing preferences should be phased out over a period of time.
2. We should like to see trade in the widest possible range of agricultural commodities and foodstuffs regulated by moderate fixed tariffs.
Moderate duties constitute the simplest nondiscriminatory method of
regulating trade.
3. Nontariff barriers should be reduced.

Almost as Freeman spoke, the Agricultural Council of the European
Community authorized a raise in the uniform gate price levy on
poultry products from 13 to 42 percent. This set off the "chicken war"
which from the start, most observers felt, the United States was bound
to lose. Beginning in the late 1950s several large broiler producers in
the United States opened a lucrative market, particularly in Germany
and Italy. The trade jumped from around $13 million in 1958 to more
than $56 million in 1963. The increased imports of poultry jeopardized
the domestic markets of several large interests in Germany, Italy,
France, and the Netherlands where the broiler industry (in some cases
through license arrangements with enterprises in the United States) was
beginning to develop. The whole controversy was pitched in the
name of the small poultry producers of the United States and the protection of the small farm flocks of Europe. The fact was that with the
possible exception of some corporation in the United States, which included small farmers, few small farmers were involved. The U.S. producers were mainly very large corporations which controlled the pat-
ented baby chicks and furnished the credit and feed to the farmer; he
served as little more than a caretaker for the enterprise. To put the
situation another way, between 1954 and 1958 the United States exported an average of 44.5 million pounds of poultry products. Using
this as an index of 100, the figures rose steadily from an index of 182.7
in 1958–59 to 694 in 1961–62. In terms of pounds, the figure was 309
million, nearly eight times the 1954–58 import. When protests and
negotiations failed to change the Common Market ruling, the U.S. government, consistent with the warning of Secretary Freeman, suspended

tariff preferences on a variety of products imported from Common Market countries. The main products affected were brandy from France and automobile trucks valued at $1,000 or more from Germany. The rates for brandy under the most-favored-nation treatment had been $1.00–$1.25 per gallon; these were raised to the statutory limit of $5.00 per gallon. On vehicles the most-favored-nation rate was 8.5 percent; this was raised to 25 percent. While these increases were substantial, they did not materially affect the volume of such imports into the United States, except on Volkswagen trucks which dropped from a dollar volume of $15.7 million in 1960 to $2.7 million in 1968. Americans who wanted high-quality brandy or a Volkswagen truck were willing to pay the extra charge. Europeans, however, were unwilling to pay premium prices for American chickens. The value of poultry exports to Europe plummeted from the high of some $66 million to less than $10 million; now, twelve years later and after special efforts to re-capture some of the market, it is at $14 million, including eggs. How-ever, the effect of this high tariff on internal production in Europe was predictable. Poultry production in West Germany jumped from 17,000 tons in 1960 to 120,000 tons in 1968, with the result that Germany has a surplus to export to neighboring countries such as Sweden and Greece. Some of the levy money collected from imports is used to sub-sidize the exports of surplus poultry. Action in other areas was no less shocking as it became evident that the managers of the Common Market were interpreting the treaty provisions on freer trade to mean that "free trade is all right so long as it does not embarrass any member politically while dealing with its farmer constituents." Other actions by the Commission caused concern if not shock to U.S. trade and govern-ment officials. The levies on grains and wheat in the Netherlands were raised from 87 cents to 90.6 cents per bushel and in West Germany from $1.16 to $1.67 per bushel. The levy on corn was raised in the Nether-lands from 42.3 cents to 47.3 cents per bushel, in West Germany from $1.17 to $1.40. Wheat flour was raised from 69.9 cents to $2.25 per hundred-pound bag. In 1966 poultry products, grains, and wheat flour represented nearly half of all U.S. farm products sold abroad for dollars. The protectionist policy of the Common Market is a genuine threat to U.S. agriculture.

Between the creation of the Common Market in 1958 and the beginning of the Common Agricultural Policy in 1962, agricultural trade between the United States and each of the Six was on a bilateral basis; tariffs, regulations, quotas, and quality regulations in force under previous trade negotiations and commercial treaties applied. Because of shorter crops in Europe and an intense trade drive on the part of the United States, exports to the Common Market showed a steady climb. Using the 1957–59 trade period as an index of 100, U.S. agri-cultural exports climbed from an index of 116.2 to 121.7 at the end of the transition period. In terms of dollars, this was an increase from

$946 million in the 1957-59 period to $1,099 million in 1960, $1,157 million in 1961, and for 1962, when the Common Agricultural Policy began, $1,151 million. At present, at the end of the transition period, the rate of increase has slowed and actually declined somewhat, but the figure is still more than $1.4 billion.

All Common Market countries shared in this increase except France where the dollar volume held steady for the period. In terms of the percentage of agricultural exports to individual countries, West Germany ranked first with an average of 32 percent of all U.S. exports, the Netherlands next with 30 percent, Italy 17.5 percent, Belgium and Luxembourg 10.9 percent, and France 8 percent. It is apparent that the increased levies on wheat and feed grains, the attendant price increases, and above all the price stability have prompted increased plantings of soft wheat and corn in France, South Germany, and Italy. United States farmers generally have shared handsomely in the rising affluence of the European Community and still retain a large and important sector of the external agricultural trade. However, they should not be without some serious concern for the future. While the poultry war is well known, less known is the virtual collapse of any bread grain market for U.S. soft wheat in the Six.[1] If current trade statistics mean anything, there are disturbing signs on the feed grain front. An example is grain sorghum, a new and important export crop. Until recently the U.S. exports of this crop had been growing year by year, reaching a total of 266 million bushels in 1967. Then exports dropped to 150 million bushels in 1968, and to less than 125 million bushels in 1969. Dock strikes in 1969 were responsible for the short-term loss, but rising competition of other grains and production increases in the Six of 5.7 million tons of coarse grains in the past three years are mainly responsible for the major decline. Imports of such grains have decreased by 3.4 million tons. Wheat production has increased in the same period by 4 million tons, developing a substantial surplus of soft wheat which is sold in third-country markets in competition with U.S. wheat.

As President Richard Nixon began his European tour early in 1969, rumors and plans were circulating in the Common Market which would seriously threaten the annual $500 million soybean market the United States enjoyed. The United States had scored a victory in the Kennedy Round by having soybeans (and several other items traditionally entering Europe duty free) bound for the indefinite future. But by the late 1960s the Community, burdened by mounting surpluses of butter and seeking ways to reduce output, had focused on the idea of placing a special tax on oilseeds. Soybean oil is one of the principal ingredients of margarine, and oilseed meal is an important feed for dairy cattle. The tax of some $60 per ton on soybeans would make

---

1. Dollar value of grain exports was $327 million in 1969–70 against $708 million in 1965–66.

margarine more expensive, and the new managers of the Six hoped this would cause consumers to buy less margarine and more higher-priced butter, thereby holding down the butter surpluses. By the same token, high dairy feed prices discourage the expansion of dairy herds and might actually reduce the number of dairy cattle. This assault on the butter surplus problem, if carried out, not only would have nullified the effect of the favorable tariff position the United States had obtained in the Kennedy Round but would have set up another nontariff device which would decrease or at least make more difficult the international agricultural trade the Kennedy Round was supposed to encourage.

The managers of the Common Market are now planning similar moves for tobacco and tobacco products, working on several devices to cut down their surplus production without resorting to the U.S. practice of direct intervention in planting and land use. These schemes constituted one of the major problems for the Nixon administration as attempts were made to improve relations with Europe. The problem now, as in the past, is to reconcile the absolute necessity for continuing and expanding trade with the pressures for more protection that are bound to develop as the production capacity of many countries goes beyond the normal requirements of home use. Probably one-sixth of the income from farm operations in this country is at stake in the way this question is resolved.

Chapter 5

THE EUROPEAN FREE TRADE ASSOCIATION

UNDER SOME PRESSURE from the United States 17 West European countries, recipients of Marshall Plan funds in the European Recovery program, organized the Organization for European Economic Cooperation (OEEC) in 1948.[1] The purpose was to coordinate the recovery
program and where possible make better use of the total resources of
the area in the restoration of Europe after World War II. Paramount
in the discussions of this group were agricultural production and a
liberalized trade policy that would facilitate the transfer of resources
between member countries as an aid to recovery. Under a convention
signed in Paris December 14, 1960, the member countries of OEEC with
the addition of the United States and Canada became the Organization
for Economic Cooperation and Development (OECD). Japan was added
in 1961.

Objectives set out by the convention were

To achieve the highest sustainable economic growth.

To contribute to sound economic expansion of member and nonmember countries.

To contribute to the expansion of world trade on a multilateral
nondiscriminatory basis in accordance with international obligations.

In the months before and after the signing of the Treaty of Rome,

---

1. Austria, Belgium, Denmark, France, the Federal Republic of Germany, Greece,
Iceland, Ireland, Italy, Luxembourg, the Netherlands, Norway, Portugal, Sweden,
Switzerland, Turkey, and the United Kingdom.

34

Great Britain had led a move by Western European countries outside the Six to establish a broadened free-trade area without the political and economic integration called for in the Common Market agreement. Various committees of OEEC negotiating for such an arrangement issued a memorandum in October 1958, reaffirming the determination to put an expanded free-trade agreement into force in January 1959. However, in a press statement in November 1958, the French government announced that it did not seem possible to establish a free-trade area as had been proposed, and that the French government was looking for a new solution. Further negotiations were suspended at that time.

The United Kingdom had declined to join the nations involved in the European Coal and Steel Community on grounds that membership would limit her sovereignty and violate her traditional arrangements with the Commonwealth countries and territories. The same argument was offered for not joining the Six in the creation of the Common Market. Neutral countries also showed reluctance to accept full membership in the Common Market, contending that they would lose their political neutrality. Other Western European countries felt they could not achieve the economic and social adjustments required by membership.

Origin

With the breakdown of efforts to establish a larger free-trade area within the OEEC, several of the member countries continued to explore ways of countering the European Community (EC). Some considered setting up an economic and trade program that would compete with the Common Market. Seven of these countries, led by Great Britain, organized the European Free Trade Association (EFTA). The convention to establish the association was initiated in Stockholm in November 1959, and the instruments of ratification were deposited on May 3, 1960. By the Stockholm Convention, the member states—Britain, Denmark, Norway, Sweden, Austria, Switzerland, and Portugal—bound themselves to establish a free market in industrial products by the abolition of tariffs and other obstacles to trade over a period of ten years. They pledged to remove trade barriers even more quickly if the situation proved feasible.[2] Each country, however, remained free to decide its own tariff with countries that were not signatories of the agreement. Rules were laid down to prevent goods originating in nonmember countries from coming into a low-tariff country and then being exported duty free to other countries of the association. It should be noted that the convention dealt with industrial goods only; agricul-

---

2. Free trade in industrial products was achieved in 1966, two years ahead of the Common Market.

ture was to have special treatment. The first tariff reduction on in
dustrial goods, amounting to 20 percent, took place in July 1960; it
was followed by a 10 percent reduction in 1961 and an agreement to
cut quantitative restrictions by 20 percent on July 1 of each year. The
industrial tariffs and restrictions were steadily reduced in the following
year and were totally eliminated on January 1, 1967—ahead of the
scheduled date of 1970. Finland became an associate member in 1961.
Iceland joined as an associate in 1970.

The overhead structure of the Outer Seven, as the original membership of EFTA is frequently called, is far different from the large
bureaucracy at Brussels which manages the affairs of the Common
Market. The Outer Seven has a council of ministers in which each
member state has one vote. The council can meet either at the foreign
office level or at the relevant minister level, and it can make decisions
binding on all states. Decisions and recommendations on new obligations are by unanimous vote, routine administrative changes by
majority vote. Subordinate committees of experts deal with specific
problems. A secretariat and a Secretary General are maintained in
Geneva.

Special Arrangements for Agriculture

Article 22 of the Stockholm Convention recognized that special
arrangements were needed to expand agricultural trade and provide
reasonable reciprocity to those member states whose economies depended to a great extent on agricultural exports. This could be done
by agreement of the group as a whole or by special arrangements between individual member states. As an example, Great Britain made
an agreement with Denmark whereby British tariffs on Danish bacon,
canned pork, luncheon meat, blue cheese, and canned cream were
eliminated. Other arrangements have been made by EFTA countries
on citrus from Spain, and a wide variety of restrictions on the movement
of agricultural products between member countries of EFTA have
been removed. The convention further provided that some outside the
Seven could negotiate with any of the Seven for special arrangements
on categories of goods or total trade. The first such arrangement with
an outside state was with Finland in March 1961. The principle
behind the agreement was to create free trade between the Outer Seven
and that country. Accordingly, the agreement provided for progressive
abolition of customs duties and import restrictions; there was a timetable with special allowances for the specific conditions of the Finnish
economy.

In April 1964 the United States and the United Kingdom entered
into an agreement on market sharing for grains. Through this agreement U.S. grain farmers were guaranteed that grain exports to the

United Kingdom would not fall below the 1964 level. They were also guaranteed a proportionate share of the British market as it grew larger. The agreement covered wheat, flour, and major feed grains. Provisions were made for protest and corrective action in the event that British imports from the United States should fall below the level of the average for the three previous years. The agreement also took into consideration the other major suppliers of grain to the United Kingdom. All suppliers were assured that prices would not be allowed to drop below a specified minimum price, and they were to participate in an annual review of the program. World market prices did not drop below the minimum during the period of the agreement; in most years it averaged above the minimum. The scheme divided British grain imports among the traditional suppliers and guaranteed to British farmers the remainder of the market and an assured price for a "standard quantity." The "standard quantity" system means that the domestic producers receive a lower per unit return if production exceeds this standard. If, as an example, the standard quantity required only 90 percent of production, the reduction in the unit payment would be 10 percent. (British farmers are paid a sum equal to the difference between import prices and costs of domestic production.) The general agreement by the United Kingdom and its suppliers was viewed as a model during the preparations for the Kennedy Round of tariff negotiations. However, as will be noted in Chapter 8, this pattern did not prevail in the GATT negotiations.

More than a dozen special bilateral arrangements exist between EFTA members and outside countries. If, as in most cases, the bilateral agreement involves states that are members of GATT, the accord is applicable to other members of GATT. Most of the agreements have a special clause dealing with dumped or subsidized agricultural products. Also, most agreements provide for elimination of tariffs on some items.

Article 22 of the Stockholm Convention places an obligation upon EFTA members to pursue agricultural policies in a manner that takes into account the interests of the other member states. It further requires EFTA countries to pay due regard to the continuation of traditional trade with non-EFTA countries. What the legalistic jargon of the convention and the supportive policy documents really say is that EFTA countries agree to promote trade in agricultural products among themselves while maintaining full authority over their individual country's agricultural policies.

A large number of processed and manufactured products based on agriculture and not subject to the industrial section of the convention were placed in a special treatment list. One section of the convention (Section D of Article 21) gives the council authority to delete any given product from the special agricultural list, thus transferring it to the industrial list and subjecting it to tariff reduction. All tariffs on intra-area trade in industrial products have been removed. The list of items deleted from the special treatment list is growing as production and trade policies of the member states become more harmonized. It should be noted, however, that the same provisions against subsidized exports in the industrial section of EFTA apply to agriculture. The principal device for harmonizing and integrating the intra-area trade production and trade policies in agricultural goods of the member states, as well as outside trade policy, is the Annual Review of Trade undertaken by the council. The purpose of the review is to determine whether the main EFTA objective—to facilitate the expansion of trade—is being fulfilled. In addition to the tariffs on agricultural products in intra-area trade, there are many export taxes, special transportation rates, border taxes, quotas, and seasonal restrictions to consider. The earlier reviews dealt almost exclusively with trade problems; in the 1967–68 review the effects of structural changes and price policies on production and the relationship between expected output and market opportunities in EFTA were stressed.

STRUCTURAL CHANGES

The annual review in 1966 noted a series of important structural and market changes in agriculture. Austria was able to report land consolidation (grouping small holdings into one piece through a cooperative effort of farmers in a given area) of some 16,000 hectares per year. Enlargement of holdings in Austria (consolidating two or more individual farms into a single farm) was taking place at the rate of some 20,000 hectares a year. Denmark had boosted the amount of funds used in support of its Agricultural Products Marketing Act and had abolished levies on beef and veal imported for home consumption. Danish policy on import of fruits and vegetables had been liberalized. Danish exports to the EC had increased by 2 percent in 1966 over the previous year, and trade with outside countries had increased by 24 percent. Finland had abolished subsidies on fertilizer production and drastically reduced programs for land reclamation. Norway had fixed agricultural prices and subsidies at a level in a design to increase farm income and inaugurated a major program of road building, drainage, and pasture improvement. Portugal had launched a program to improve the quality of products which had resulted in an increase in farm wages by 16 percent. Sweden, sometimes burdened with surpluses in meat and dairy products, had launched an agricultural project designed to bring better balance to the total economy and to make the country 80 percent self-sufficient on a calorie basis. There had been some liberalization on access to the Swedish market for certain products, chiefly fruits and vegetables from countries outside EFTA. Switzerland, a major importer of grains but an important exporter of dairy products, had reduced subsidies on butter and cheese production and lowered the retail price in order to increase home consumption. Quantitative restrictions were eliminated for mutton and lamb. The United Kingdom, largest importer of agricultural products in EFTA and one of the largest in the world, had made no significant changes in policy. The value of agricultural goods imported from EFTA countries by the United Kingdom rose by 7 percent in 1966, but the exports of certain agricultural specialty products of small base volume had risen by 61 percent. There is no doubt that this association of seven important European states has resulted in a marked increase in trade not only of industrial but also of agricultural products.

PRESENT STATUS

At present EFTA is a free-trade area of nine countries with a market of 100 million people. Trade statistics show remarkable gains in both exports and imports in almost every category of trade and with every trading area except the United States. Figures for the six years prior to the formation of EFTA, 1953–59, compared with those of the six-year period 1959–66, show total EFTA exports to the world increased by 27 percent. Exports between members were boosted more than 72 percent. Exports to the EC went up 23.4 percent, while exports to the United States were down 14.7 percent. For the same periods imports from the world increased by 33 percent; intra-EFTA imports increased 76.2 percent; imports from EC were a bare 5.2 percent. The import figure from the United States was a whopping 32.2 percent increase against a deficit export in the pre-EFTA period.[3]

A study of trade developments during 1969 showed that total trade in EFTA was higher than in 1968, a peak year which also showed an accelerating rate. Total imports of EFTA countries in 1969 were $43,939 million and exports were $38,215 million—11 and 15 percent respectively higher than in 1968. Trade among the seven member countries and two associate members was 17 percent higher than during the previous year and for the first time was in excess of $10 billion. Exports to EC were buoyant—up 18.5 percent over 1968. Imports from the Six were 12 percent higher. Trade with the United States in 1969 was low, up only 1.5 percent, after a high figure in 1968. Imports from the United States were low with a gain of only 7.5 percent over the year before.[4] The release of this study permitted a look at EFTA after ten years in terms of total development and, to some extent, effects. There had been total free trade in industrial goods during three years of EFTA history. Total imports for EFTA countries during the ten-year

3. Statistics taken from official report of the European Free Trade Association publications issued in Washington in February 1968.
4. From the EFTA Washington office issued March 1970.

period rose 108 percent and exports rose 111 percent. There had been no substantial tariff cuts during seven of the years. In the last three years (free-trade years) EFTA showed an increase of 186 percent—nearly triple the 1959 figure. In the area of trade with outside countries or groups, the increase of exports and imports with the EC was 130 percent, and imports from the United States in this three-year period were up 135 percent. European Free Trade Association business with EC countries in 1969 was $2 billion in each direction, an increase of 10 percent over 1968.

It would be presumptuous to argue that the mere removal of tariffs on industrial goods was responsible for all the rather healthy growth in trade shown by the above figures. However, it is generally accepted that much of the growth has been the result of EFTA, along with a better economic climate and increased mutual confidence in the trade policies of each country. The improved atmosphere resulted from the frequent and continuing studies by EFTA members on how to remove more of the barriers and to establish "better rules of the game." It resulted also from a sincere desire to make the system work. The members have forbidden themselves the flagrant practice widely used throughout the world of enacting nontariff restrictions which cancel the effect of tariff cuts. They refrain also from giving direct government aid or bonuses to exporters thereby creating domestic and international problems.

COUNCIL FOR MUTUAL ECONOMIC ASSISTANCE

Almost simultaneous with the creation of the Common Market and the organization of the European Free Trade Association, Eastern Europe under the leadership of Russia was quickly organized (on paper at least) into a similar integrated trade system called the Council for Mutual Economic Assistance (CMEA).[5] The CMEA agreements between the Eastern European countries, including East Germany and Russia, were bilateral. There was also a general freeing of trade restrictions between each of the states in the group and establishment of a common exchange and trade system. It was visualized that this trading bloc would eventually act in unison on matters of trade and tariff, money, transportation, and distribution of resources. Some observers predicted that two gigantic trading blocs would develop: Eastern European countries associated with Russia carrying out the political, economic, and social views and principles of communism; in the West another bloc which would champion the ideas of Western democracy and capitalism. Since 1948 a great deal of U.S. policy development centered on this idea and possibility. Only in the last four or five years

5. Russia, East Germany, Poland, Czechoslovakia, Romania, Hungary, Bulgaria, Albania. Yugoslavia refused to become a member.

has there been any significant relaxation of trade and economic relations by the United States with Eastern Europe.

FUTURE OF EFTA

With the United Kingdom and three of her partners in EFTA in the process of becoming full members of the EC with all that this implies, what is the future of EFTA? In discussions with EFTA members as late as 1968, when EFTA had proved to be a beneficial development for all of the members, one gained the impression that it was never regarded as a permanent grouping. Rather it was a spin-off from the EC; most members hoped for an expanded European Community with perhaps some alleviation of the rigid requirements for full membership. Great Britain, after reconsideration of its earlier refusal to join with the original Six, had by 1960 applied for full membership (see Chapter 6).

The feeling persisted throughout Europe during the Common Market transition period that sooner or later the European Community would be enlarged. Paul Henri Spaak, Belgian Foreign Minister and one of the moving spirits for a United Europe and a leader in the Common Market, warned in February 1965 that "there is a real danger that the two organizations will develop separately and that the gap between them will widen." However, with the second French veto in 1967 of Britain's entry to the Market, the British government announced it would not withdraw its application to membership. George Brown, then Foreign Secretary in the Labour government, said:

We continue to believe the long-term interests of this country and of Europe require that we should become members of the European Community. We now propose to enter into consultations with the five members of the European Community who supported the Commission's view that negotiations should be started at an early stage. We shall, of course, be in close touch with the European Free Trade Association and the Irish Republic. We are by no means the only country whose hopes for progress toward a genuine European unity have been temporarily disappointed.

The faith of Brown was justified by the action of the Council of Ministers meeting at the Hague, December 1 and 2, 1969. Here for the first time they unanimously agreed to "begin negotiations with Great Britain and other applicant states and to make immediate preparations." By June 1970 the Six had reached a common negotiating position on problems such as the length of the transition period, the Commonwealth, differences between Great Britain's and the Community's agricultural policies (Britain by its application had accepted the Common Agriculture Policy), the kind of monetary system to be followed, and British contribution to the Community budget.

Negotiations by the new Conservative government of the United

Kingdom began in mid 1970 and culminated in the final agreement on the details of British membership June 22, 1971, in Luxembourg. This was, as Chief British Negotiator Godfrey Rippon put it, "the end of the beginning." The actual ending came after a frenzied and politically explosive campaign by the British Conservative government to win parliamentary approval of the final and momentous step which will make Great Britain an integral part of Europe. In the future Frenchmen and Germans and Italians will legislate on economic matters for Britain, and Britain and her three partners in the new Community of ten will have a voice in the legislation affecting the other six members.

One of the early concerns of Great Britain and her three applicant partners was what would happen to the other members of EFTA which—for reasons of sovereignty, neutral status, or treaty obligations— could not become full members of the European Community. This was a very strong issue in the original British application by the Macmillan government in 1961. Pierre Harmel, Belgian Foreign Minister and President of the Council of Ministers, speaking for the Council on June 30, 1970, stated:

> The Community is prepared to open discussions with the European States which are members of the EFTA, but which have not applied for membership, with a view to seeking solutions to the problems raised by the enlargement. The agreements concluded by these discussions would be binding upon the enlarged community.

In the interim period since the negotiating position of the Six was announced, each of the EFTA countries remaining outside full membership has sought special arrangements for an association with the enlarged community. Sweden, carefully surveying its traditional neutrality, appears to be on the verge of seeking full membership (see Chapter 16).

Chapter 6

BRITAIN AND THE COMMON MARKET

IN WHAT HISTORY will surely record as one of the great turning points in her relations with the world, the British Parliament in October 1971 (by a split vote in the major parties) took the final irrevocable step to join the Common Market. Implicit in this was the decision and desire of the British people to identify directly with the future of Western Europe from the inside rather than from outside the Continent. Approval of the simple declaration "That this House approves Her Majesty's government decision in principle to join the European communities on the basis of arrangements which have been negotiated" ended, by a vote of 356 to 244, Britain's 1,000 years of independent history and established her decision to become a partner and play a role in a United Europe.

The government margin made up of both Conservative and Labour votes was 112. The House of Lords followed immediately with an approval of 451 to 58. Bonfires on both sides of the English Channel greeted the momentous vote. The six-day marathon debate came to a climax in late evening amidst dramatic crowd scenes inside and outside Parliament.

The year 1972 will be marked by other votes and dramatic scenes as Parliament realigns British laws to conform to the rules and principles of the Common Market. Among the changes will be a reversal of the British agricultural policy, already in process, which replaces the deficiency payment system of aiding agriculture with higher con-

43

...... points, thus obtaining farm subsidies from the marketplace rather than from the treasury.[1]

This turn toward Europe abandons the idea of a globe-girdling Commonwealth and reduces the special privileges of the Commonwealth countries. It admittedly weakens if it does not abandon the special relationship with the United States.

The act on which the curtain fell in October 1971 came as something of an anticlimax to a long and winding journey that started in 1961 when the Conservative government, led by Prime Minister Harold Macmillan, applied for membership in the Common Market. The Labour government, led by Harold Wilson, at that time opposed joining the Common Market. When they came into power in 1964, they reversed their decision and sought admission.

During the debate on accession in 1971, this time under a Conservative government, Wilson was again almost but not quite the loyal opposition. His speeches, probably in deference to the strong resistance of some of his trade union members to joining the Market, hinted strongly at outright opposition but never quite reached that point. He opposed the terms of admission, not the membership. His own party was split: his deputy party leader Roy Jenkins and his chief negotiator during Labour party's rule, George Thomson, voted with the Conservatives, as did other Labour members. British public opinion polls, which had shown nearly 60 percent opposition in June at the end of the negotiations, had climbed to a nearly 50–50 split in October.

What took place between the beginning of formal negotiations with the Six in mid-1970 and the final vote in Parliament in 1971 reads almost like a cliff-hanger movie script. The final turning point probably came in May 1971 in the meeting between Tory Prime Minister Edward Heath and Georges Pompidou, President of France, when agreement was reached on the kind of European unity and the monetary system likely to be achieved in the years ahead. Heath returned from that meeting with sails billowing at the prospect of early and successful conclusion to the negotiations at Luxembourg. In a ten-minute speech to a packed House of Commons he proclaimed: "The divisions and suspiciously between Britain and France are gone. We agree that Britain should be a part of an enlarged community and a partner in the building of a united Europe." He gave assurances that joining the Community did not entail loss of national identity or erosion of essential national sovereignty.

As Heath predicted, less than one month later the negotiators in Luxembourg, after two all-night sessions and at 5:30 in the morning,

---

1. As early as 1968 qualified British economists argued that inevitably more of the British subsidy to agriculture would have to come out of the marketplace instead of the treasury. Levies were increased on certain imported agricultural items in 1969, and since that time there has been a gradual reduction of treasury subsidies and increased prices in the marketplace. Presumably the change will be complete shortly after the transition period for joining the Market ends in 1975.

announced agreement on the final troublesome issues then pending—
protection of New Zealand butter, a compromise on Commonwealth
sugar producers, and Britain's portion of the Guarantee and Guidance
Fund.[2] It was ironic that in the final round three essentially agricultural
issues had overshadowed the infinitely bigger issues of monetary system
and centralized power over national budgets inherent in the Common
Market system.

REASONS FOR JOINING

Prime Minister Heath's speech in Commons June 23 gave the
government's reasons for joining the European Community.

Britain must join the European Community now. She must realize
that she is catching up with the train. The train can neither
stop nor change its destination. The future of Great Britain is
to be on that train.

Since 1961 successive governments have taken the view that membership in the European Community is a necessity if Britain's
security and prosperity are to be preserved.

The terms negotiated are right for Britain, the costs bearable, and
the advantages manifest.

All of the Commonwealth partners have been safeguarded in the
agreements negotiated.

World peace will be enhanced by the fullest possible unity of
Europe.

There is no question of any erosion of essential national sovereignty
in Common Market membership; what is involved is sharing
and enlargement of individual national sovereignties in the
general interest.

Britain as a member of the Community will share in the decisions
from inside the Market which will affect her and the entire
world.

---

2. The Guarantee and Guidance Fund is used principally to subsidize exports of
surplus farm products and pay for structural change in farming, purchases, and storage
of surplus commodities within the Market. The fund, presently made up from levies
on imported agricultural products and contributions from each member state of the
Six, will after 1977 also receive funds from other customs duties and the value-added tax
system. The United Kingdom argued during the negotiations that, as the largest importer of food products, she would pay the highest amount into the fund and receive
little in return; France, Ireland, and Denmark as surplus producers would receive most
of the money. She objected to an assessment for the fund based on gross national product. Britain admitted that her share of the customs duties on other products and the
value-added tax were equitable but fought hard for a compromise on the agricultural
levies. The final figures to become effective in 1978 will place the contribution of
Britain at 19.19 percent of the total community budget with a promise that this will
be reviewed after three years of operation.

1961–71

With the die cast at last, perhaps it is worthwhile to retrace some of the road which Great Britain has traveled since the eventful decisions in 1961 and to highlight some of the implications of this momentous change in the course of history.

The Macmillan government in 1961, while accepting the basic objectives and provisions of the Treaty of Rome, asked the Six to grant Britain special treatment on some matters which would enable her to meet particular situations. These special conditions were outlined in a talk by Edward Heath, then Lord Privy Seal, to the Minister's Council of the Six in October 1961. Heath stated that satisfactory solutions would have to be found for three problems: Commonwealth trade, United Kingdom agriculture, and the European Free Trade Association (EFTA). Of these issues, agriculture presented the most perplexing domestic problem. Great Britain and the Six shared the common objectives of protecting the income of agricultural producers and at the same time providing consumers with adequate food at reasonable prices. The United Kingdom was ready to participate with the Six in a common agricultural policy, Heath said, but there would have to be some way of reconciling the system of support to agriculture used by the Six with that used in the United Kingdom. Specifically, the United Kingdom would have to consider with the Six how the interests of British farmers and horticulturists could be effectively safeguarded, and any changes in the British system would take time. On the issues of internal and external tariffs Great Britain was ready to negotiate uniform cuts. "None of the non-commercial provisions of the treaty would cause any difficulty," Heath argued.

The Labour party (then out of power) opposed EC membership for Britain, but the most important reason full membership was not acquired was the threat of a French veto. Most observers believed that French President Charles de Gaulle promised to veto any formal application on political grounds. It is unlikely, however, that others of the Six would have accepted the United Kingdom on terms and conditions which the Macmillan government demanded.

With the rise of the Labour party to power in 1964, Prime Minister Harold Wilson presided over a reversal of his party's position on the Common Market. In 1966 Britain once again applied for membership. This time Britain softened her position of special treatment for the Commonwealth and special arrangements for protecting farmers; the Labour government was willing to pay the price of admission on EC terms.

Why Great Britain, in the first instance, made the tacit admission that her global power and imperial position had declined and staked her future on becoming a genuine political and economic partner in Europe, and why France twice vetoed the British application only to later reverse her position, are issues which historians will argue about in the decades ahead. However, it was apparent to the outside world and surely to Britain herself that the future of this once mighty empire lay in becoming a real part of Europe. Prime Minister Wilson gave an indication of his awareness of this reality when he said in 1966 that "the pattern of a new Europe will be intricately cut in the next two decades and Britain must not be left among the scraps on the cutting floor." Although the second bid was shunted aside (not actually vetoed by France), Britain approached the EC in a far less rigid mood than in the first round six years before. It was, one might say, a different Britain speaking. The Macmillan government of 1961 still considered itself a member of the Big Three powers which had won World War II and still clung to the Churchillian dream of empire and superpower directing the peace of the world. Macmillan and President John F. Kennedy had just completed the "Nassau agreements" which reaffirmed Britain's special relationship with the United States. Britain came away from Nassau with access to U.S. atomic weapons development and some Polaris missiles at a cut price. These global pretensions and special relationships with the United States, perhaps as much as anything else, provoked the first French veto. When the second was threatened, the picture in Europe had radically changed. France already had refused to participate in the so-called European Defense Community and was pulling further away from NATO. The French were developing their own rocket and missile system and had embarked on an international effort to return the major currencies of the world to the gold standard. The American hope of gaining access to the larger economic community through Great Britain and the American assumption that West Germany would be the strongest and most appropriate military power around which to build a Western defense community were eroding fast. West Germany was refusing to be a U.S. satellite and had begun to seek limited economic ties and diplomatic relations with the East. Great Britain, still clinging verbally to her special relationship with the United States, yearned for a more independent role. British and German attitudes were increasingly in tune with the rest of Western Europe and looked to the formation of a European community which would be neither dependent on nor dominated by Washington.

One European observer, discussing the French opposition to British membership and recalling the attitude of European states in the Kennedy Round negotiations, said, "We are afraid of almost everybody but the United States. The United States is so large, so powerful, and has so many self-imposed obligations in the rest of the world that almost any of us can twist the nose of Uncle Sam with impunity."

If, as most analysts assume, the first French veto was dictated largely by political considerations and a desire to remain the strongest partner in the Common Market, what were the elements that dictated the second threatened veto? The British had come, while far from hat in hand, apparently ready to loosen old Commonwealth trade ties and scuttle some of the earlier preconditions. Britain was ready to join with no strings attached. George Brown, British Foreign Secretary, presented the new view in mid-1967 before the ministerial meeting of the Western European union. He said bluntly, "Britain now asks to join you. We want to link our efforts with yours." Brown pointed to the technical contribution Britain could make to the Six and to a growing unity of economic and political purposes which would enable "Greater Europe" to play a full part in world affairs.

Europe technologically will find itself in the 1970's producing equipment of the 1960's unless the resources and technologies of the whole are mobilized so as to keep pace with stronger aggregations of industrial power. We believe this greater Europe can emerge as a community expressing its own point of view and influence in world affairs, not only in the commercial and economic, but also in the political and defense fields. There is nothing in our law and practice which is irreconcilable with Community requirements. Many of the necessary adaptations can be made without delay after a 12-month transitional period, but some of the changes we will be called upon to make, particularly in agriculture, will be very considerable, and an adequate period of adaptation will be needed.

At a later meeting in Brussels, French representatives said that "France in principle welcomes British membership to the Common Market, but the United Kingdom must meet certain requirements—in France's view—before serious negotiations might begin." These requirements, implied or spelled out by President de Gaulle and his Foreign Minister, were:

1. Political detachment from the United States.
2. Commercial detachment from the Commonwealth.
3. Proof of secure balance of payments.
4. Abandonment of the pound sterling's role as reserve currency.
5. Acceptance of a European consensus on monetary reform.
6. Adopting in practice as well as principle the Common Agricultural Policy.
7. A start on Europeanization of the British social services and economic policies.

This was a formidable list, and it would be difficult for Britain to accept in principle, must less to implement. Again membership was denied by the threat of a French veto. Instead of withdrawing the application as she had done in 1963, Great Britain began negotiations with five of the Six who were anxious that she become a partner. These talks covered a wide range of possible new relationships between Britain and the continental nations: a free trade area, an associate membership for Britain in the EC, a loose customs union, a more formal association of the Community nations with EFTA. Finally, in the closing days of 1969, changes in the political and military situation brought about a series of critical sessions within the Six. The meeting of the Council of Ministers at the Hague in December 1969 is regarded by most Europeans as the major start toward the enlarged Community and some form of a more unified Europe. Not only was the decision in principle to begin negotiations for the admission of Great Britain to the Market made, but other fundamental questions were resolved—at least in principle. France had softened her stand and conditions for the admission of Britain. President Georges Pompidou said in an interview on December 15: "We are delighted to welcome Britain to Europe." The Hague conference had proved his sincerity when he declared there that France would not veto admission of Britain to the Community.

New Concept for Community

The Hague conference and the agreement to begin negotiations in June 1970 for admission of Great Britain gave a new impetus to the whole Community concept and resulted in action on several important issues that had been stalled for two years. Commission President Jean Rey, in his report to the European Parliament on December 11, 1969, characterized the results as impressive and listed four important developments: (1) a regulation harmonizing social security benefits for migrant workers; (2) a common commercial policy regulation; (3) unblocking of international negotiations with Austria, Yugoslavia, Spain, and Israel; (4) formal merger of Euratom with the other bodies of the European Community.

When the formal talks between the Six and the United Kingdom got under way in mid-1971, three of the basic goals of the European Community as set out in the Treaty of Rome concerned Great Britain most: (1) the Common Agricultural Policy, (2) a common monetary policy, (3) the final form of European unity. Of the three, the Common Agricultural Policy was of the most immediate concern. Where did British farm interests stand on agricultural integration? Probably the best barometer aside from the views in principle expressed by the Foreign Office was the National Farmer's Union of England, Scotland, and Ireland. The position of the union in the first British bid on the Common Agricultural Policy of the Six argued for substitution of the British system of compensatory payments for the levy systems in the Market. However, in November 1966 a Farmer's Union white paper accepted the fact that Great Britain would have to enter the European Community under the Common Agricultural Policy levy system.

In the second British bid the union tried to draw attention to what the acceptance of the Common Agricultural Policy would cost British consumers. The union had reconciled itself to the fact that Britain sooner or later would become a member of the Community and accept Community terms. Once in the Community, the union no doubt hoped to modify the agricultural and monetary policies over the years.

The union argued that the high price of cereal grain was a key not only to bread costs but to costs of all products in which grain was used. These high prices, argued the union, would result in the destruction of Britain's rather well balanced system of grains, livestock, poultry, dairy, and horticulture as farmers expanded production of cultivated grains. The union argued, for example, that the average British farmer with modern equipment, under the Common Market, could make more money raising barley and would likely turn most of his resources to feed grain production. (British agriculture is the most mechanized in the world and ranks slightly under the United States in output per man.) This would subject the British consumer to the high internal prices and flexible levies on other products and add greatly to food prices. As Europe's largest importer, Britain would pay the largest portion of the levies. According to union estimates, the British would pay £100 million annually into the European Guarantee and Guidance Fund (see Chapter 9 for details); the increased price of cereals and its influence on meats, dairy, and poultry would raise food costs to the British consumers approximately £700 million per year. In addition, the Farmer's Union estimated, the levy bill would worsen Britain's balance of payments on the order of £400 million. Prime Minister Wilson contended that "after the transitional period, these levies would probably adversely affect the balance of payments position by only around 175 to 200 million pounds." This all assumed that the trade pattern would remain stable.

CHANGES IN TRADE PATTERN

It may not be appropriate to assume that the pattern of trade will remain stable. When the British first applied for membership in the Market in 1961 nearly half of all exports and imports came from the Commonwealth. Exports to the Commonwealth were 42.1 percent of the total export trade; imports from the Commonwealth were 38.5 percent of total imports." Exports to the United States were 9.1 percent; 14.5 percent went to the Common Market; 10.7 percent to EFTA; and 23.6 percent to the rest of the world. Great Britain's imports were 12.3 percent from the United States, 14.6 percent from the European Community (roughly a balance between exports and imports from the EC), 10.7 percent from EFTA (again a roughly balanced trade), and 24.4

3. See T. K. Warley, *Agriculture: The Cost of Joining the Common Market* (Chatham House, series 3, 1967).

percent from the rest of the world including Eastern Europe. By the end of 1969 this picture had changed considerably.

Political considerations aside, the main attraction of Great Britain to the Common Market is the outlet it provides for British industrial products. In December 1969, George Thomson, the cabinet minister principally concerned with European affairs, issued a report showing the change in the destination of British exports for the ten-year period 1958–68.[4] Exports to the Commonwealth countries had declined from 38 percent to 23 percent; exports to the EC had risen from 14 percent to 19 percent; exports to EFTA had risen from 11 percent to 14 percent; and exports to other Western European countries had risen from 2 percent to 4 percent. Collectively, Western European countries had received 27 percent of British exports in 1958 and 37 percent in 1968. At the same time, exports to the United States had risen from 9 percent to 14 percent.[5]

PROJECTIONS

The Economic Research Service of USDA has made a projection and a comparison of all agricultural imports to Great Britain up to 1975, taking into account present policies and the pattern likely to emerge when Britain becomes a member of the European Community by 1973. Since Great Britain is the world's largest importer of agricultural products and the United States is the world's largest exporter, the future market for agricultural products in the United Kingdom is of prime concern to American farmers. In 1966–67 the United States sold $454 million worth of agricultural products in the British market—the fifth largest dollar market for U.S. products. American exports to Britain exceeded Britain's purchases from the United States by $425 million, thus making a major contribution to the U.S. balance of trade. The projection and comparisons between continuance under the present policies and the entrance of Britain to the European Community are shown in dollar values in Table 6.1.

Projections for hides, wool, and skins were made separately. These imports are expected to decline sharply under the pressure of increased domestic production and declining consumption. There appears to be little difference in the imports of cotton under present policies or under the EC, since cotton is bound free entry under GATT and the price and quality of cotton offered would be the major factor in the market.

Table 6.1 indicates quite clearly that the major decline in agricultural imports when Great Britain joins the EC will be in feed grains and wheat, with some decline in meat. However, other observers, mostly in Europe, foresee a greater dislocation of British agricultural imports

4. British Information Service Paper, Dec. 1969.
5. Economic Research Service, USDA.

TABLE 6.1

	1959–63	1975 Present Policies	1976 EC Entry
		($ million)	
Meat, all kinds	1,261	1,334	1,247
Fats and oils	738	782	897
Oilseeds	996	907	961
Oilseed cake & meal	1,161	1,420	1,528
Grain equivalent	8,941	7,940	5,396
Wheat	4,542	4,115	2,948
Dried fruit	150	162	164
Other fruit equivalent	1,700	2,191	2,133
Vegetables	357	474	564

Source: USDA, Economic Research Service No. 248, July 1969.

when Britain gains full status in the EC together with Denmark, Norway, and Ireland, and if two or three Eastern European countries gain association status in the enlarged Market. They note that beef is the major deficit item in Western Europe and that practically every country in Eastern Europe is expanding its livestock industry, principally beef, in anticipation of tapping the enlarged EC market.

The Labour government which had initiated the second British bid for admission was out of office in 1970–71. The Conservative government led by Prime Minister Edward Heath carried the issue through the months of negotiations, frustrations, and compromises to the final vote in Parliament in October 1971. The full picture of what Great Britain has gained or given up in this historic move will not be known for some time.

TERMS OF ACCESSION

In the long negotiations from June 1970 to June 1971 many other critical points had been settled. The list is formidable; below are the agreements Britain and her three partners have pledged to observe:

1. Britain and other applicants accept the Treaty of Rome without reservations and all Community decisions since the foundation of the Common Market in 1958. This means free movement of goods, people, and money within the new Community of ten and adjustment of tariffs and trade agreements to the Common Market external tariff system.

2. Britain is to adjust its agriculture and agricultural trade to fit the Common Agricultural Policy. Britain will raise consumer prices to the Community level in six steps culminating in 1977.

3. The transition period for making full adjustment for both industry and agriculture is five years.

4. New members must adopt the value-added tax system, a special

type of turnover tax already in force in the Community. Britain even before negotiations had introduced legislation to adopt the value-added tax system.

5. At the end of the transition period of five years (1978) all customs duties and levies on goods coming into the Community plus a portion of the value-added tax will be paid into Community funds.

6. All African Commonwealth nations will be offered associate membership.

7. Associate membership or special trade agreements are to be offered the sugar-producing islands of the Caribbean and their interests are to be safeguarded when the Commonwealth sugar agreement runs out. The enlarged Community is to adopt a new international agreement in 1975.

8. The Common Market will guarantee outlets for 71 percent of New Zealand's dairy exports to Great Britain until 1977 when the guarantee will be abolished. However, in 1975 the dairy situation will be reexamined, looking to a world agreement on dairy products.

9. Britain's eventual share of the Community budget will be 19.19 percent. France originally insisted on 25 percent. However, in 1973 Britain will pay 8.74 of the total Community budget of $220 million. This will increase uniformly until 1977 and 18.92 percent. Two extra years will be allowed to reach the full 19.19 percent.

10. On British insistence and with concurrence of other members of the Six (especially Germany, Italy, and France), the agreement specifies that special measures might be needed to solve the problem of reasonable revenues for small farmers.

11. The Common Market fisheries policy adopted in October 1970 will be reconsidered and provisions requiring free access to all member states to fishing grounds will be amended to protect fishing rights for a limited time in some national boundaries, principally Ireland and Norway.

12. The British have pledged to gradually run down their balances of pound sterling.

With the British Parliament's acceptance of the admission conditions, the treaty of accession—which is irrevocable—was promptly ratified by the national legislatures of the Six.

It is the hope of most British leaders and the leaders of business interests outside the Community that Britain as a full member of the Community will be able to modify the highly protective and restrictive policies in agriculture which have prevailed over the transition period. It is more likely, however, that Britain will have to conform more to the Community's rules than to Britain's wishes.

Chapter 7

THE GRAND DESIGN

There is a tide in the affairs of men,
Which, taken at the flood, leads on to fortune;
Omitted, all the voyage of their life
Is bound in shallows and in miseries. . . .
We must take the current when it serves,
Or lose our ventures.

THESE LINES from Shakespeare's *Julius Caesar* may seem irrelevant to the subject under discussion. Yet the timing and context within which a new idea or pattern of national and international behavior is presented may well determine the chances of acceptance or rejection.

This feeling must have been involved when the Kennedy administration launched what became the Trade Expansion Act of 1962 and projected in global terms not only the economic and trade factors inherent in the original Reciprocal Tariff Act of June 1934 but also a vast political arrangement among the Atlantic powers. The Act of 1934 reversed the highly protective system which had culminated in the Hawley-Smoot Tariff Act of 1930, setting tariff levels at the highest point in U.S. history. Curiously, agriculture played an important role in the 1930 legislation. President Hoover wanted increased protection for farm products and a small adjustment in industrial tariffs. The Senate opted for high farm rates; the House passed a bill placing high tariffs on nearly all industrial products. In the compromise of the two measures, the highest rates on both sides were adopted. This brought quick and drastic retaliation from Western Europe, resulting in a very short time in a destructive dip in U.S. foreign trade in all products. (Something similar was predicted by

54

economists from the proposed Trade Act of 1970.) Although the Trade Expansion Act of 1962 was cast in the dull verbiage of law dealing with tariff rates, quotas, import-export levels, and the powers of the President, it incorporated two great visions: freer international trade and an Atlantic partnership with Europe against the then-solid Soviet bloc of countries of Eastern Europe. These dreams were variously called the United States–Europe patrnership, the Atlantic Community, and the Grand Design.

BACKGROUND

The new administration had the opportunity to build in a period marked by settling down, consolidation, and quiet accomplishments in the foreign field, which it inherited from the Republican administration of President Dwight Eisenhower. Following generally the policies laid down by previous administrations in the conduct of World War II and the rebuilding of Europe, the old administration had stepped down with a dawning realization that American power and influence in Europe—industrial and political—were beginning to wane.

When Kennedy took office there were both bright and gray spots for American policy around the world. The beginning of the 1960s saw Europe emerging from the economic and political chaos caused by World War II. There had been the miracle of Germany's recovery, then France's, and then Italy's, capped by attempts to unify Europe with the Coal and Steel Community, Euratom, and the Common Market. Communism had been effectively countered and contained in the West. The North Atlantic Treaty Organization (NATO) was a vast and integrated military machine and had observed its tenth anniversary. The communist-inspired Bolivian revolution had been successfully checked by early recognition and support of a new regime which moved nearer the center of the political spectrum. The seed for the Alliance for Progress in Latin America had been sown. While our past performance in the foreign field had been quietly successful, there was some concern that Americans had "gone too far." A recovered Europe, while assisted and desired by the United States, had begun to challenge some of our industrial and commercial markets. Our agriculture, once driven to the very limit to produce food for Europe, was troubled by surpluses as European farms returned to production. Our dollar balances were no longer so favorable. Cuba's Fidel Castro was causing a serious disturbance; futile efforts at a modus operandi with Russia continued in the aftermath of the Paris Conference which had been blown sky-high by the U-2 incident. A number of analysts saw the need for a new thrust in foreign affairs comparable to the high domestic aims set forth by the President in his inaugural address. There was still the illusion that perhaps this was the American century, that America had unlimited power in shaping world

events. Our policy had been to rebuild Europe and make it strong
enough to share some of the burdens of leadership in a changing world.
We had also encouraged European unity, and some of this effort was
reflected in NATO, the Common Market, and the Coal and Steel Community. By 1960 there was the prospect that Britain might become
a member of the Common Market and bring the Commonwealth and
other Western nations into the association with her. Europe thus could
be larger than any other market in the world and as a unit could be the
greatest aggregation of industrial power, military potential, commercial
enterprise, and agricultural resources in the world. This potentiality
intrigued those who felt that the economic, political, and military destiny
of the United States depended on a partnership with a European bloc
against the Soviet-dominated Communist countries. The timing then
was right for a new idea. But worthy ideas are sometimes difficult to implement. For Kennedy it was necessary either to renew the Reciprocal
Trade Agreements Act, let it die, or design a new approach and a broader
aim. Luckily for Kennedy, the decision, the will for action, and the correct time coincided. The tide was coming in, and the young, new, and
idealistic administration sought to "take the current when it serves."

In the previous administration, before the crucial decision as to
what and how issues on renewal or replacement of the Reciprocal Trade
Agreements Act should be placed before the legislative body, many op-
tions had been explored. Within the State Department, the Department
of Commerce, the Department of Agriculture, and even the White House,
various groups of career bureaucrats and outside consultants had ex-
amined the various kinds of action that could be taken when the Trade
Agreements Act expired in 1962. These study groups concluded that
the act—with its most-favored-nation clauses, peril point provisions, and
limited range of negotiable tariff reduction—should be replaced or
amended. After his election President Kennedy set up two task forces
to review the issue. One group advised letting the Trade Agreement
Act expire and then in 1963, after more time to think and plan, intro-
ducing a new trade policy which would be an integral part of foreign
policy. The other group sensed a rising tide of protectionism and advised pushing a new bill through Congress almost immediately. In
the end, each side got some satisfaction. Kennedy decided upon radical
new legislation in which trade and foreign policy would be united, and
he decided upon immediate action.

The President outlined the new legislation before many business
groups during late 1961 and early 1962. Among the first he addressed
was the National Association of Manufacturers at its annual meeting in
December 1961. This was a low-key talk to businessmen whose interests
were primarily the technical and political problems of expanding
American sales abroad and reducing competition from outside. It was
not until his speech in Independence Square, July 4, 1962, that the dar-
ing outline of the Grand Design began to emerge. In matchless rhetoric

the President pictured Britain as a future member of the Common Market along with six or seven other nations; he envisioned a Europe with unity of purpose, aims, ideals, and economics and with the United States as an equal partner. The eventual result would be an Atlantic Community, one great area of freedom based on Western democracy and the Christian-Socratic tradition. The Atlantic Community would be a great center of power, wealth, freedom, and expanding human values arrayed against the Soviet Union, Soviet-dominated Eastern Europe, and Communist China. The key sentence that day in Philadelphia was: "I will say here and now, on this day of Independence, that the United States will be ready for declaration of interdependence, that we shall be prepared to discuss the United Europe and the ways and means of forming a concrete Atlantic partnership. . . . All of this will not be finished in a year, but let the world know it is our goal."

Earlier in April 1962, Jean Monnet, one of the great architects of European unification was saying:

At this point we have now reached, Europe's economic integration is making a start toward political union possible. This continuity in action which is re-uniting Europe and transforming the West shows the capacity for progress in the free world whose leavening agent is Europe. Thus conditions permitting the gradual settlement of issues which now confront East and West will be created. When it becomes obvious to all that a United Europe and America cannot be disassociated, the goal of changing the world in accordance with only a part of mankind will have to give way to the search for true understanding. Problems that today seem insolvable may then be settled.

TRADE EXPANSION ACT OF 1962

After many committees (inside and outside the government) had conducted studies and made suggestions, President Kennedy submitted his recommendations for the Trade Expansion Act of 1962 to the Congress on January 25, 1962: "This is our greatest opportunity since the Marshall Plan to become a partner with a Europe strong enough to share with us the responsibilities and initiatives of the Free World."

In hopes of an expanding market for U.S. industrial goods and an open market for mounting agricultural surpluses, the Congress, in a rare display of unity and exuberance, acted quickly. The new legislation was signed into law July 10, 1962. Previous revisions of the Reciprocal Trade Agreements Act had dealt mainly with the time period during which the President had authority to reduce tariffs and the extent of that reduction. This new legislation gave the President much broader powers to reduce tariffs on a reciprocal basis. It also gave him power to retaliate against a nation or group of nations that treated the United States unfairly or unduly restricted trade. Realists in international trade negotiations recognized this single provision as a powerful and important tool in dealings with our Western partners.

The Act, among other things, gave the President the power for a period of five years:

1. To reduce existing tariffs by 50 percent on a reciprocal basis with any country.

2. To eliminate tariffs entirely on products in which this country and the Common Market conducted 80 percent of the world trade. This mainly concerned industrial goods produced in the United States and Europe where the two partners compete with each other.

3. To reduce or eliminate tariffs against agricultural commodities produced by underdeveloped countries of the Southern continents, provided the Common Market countries made similar concessions.

4. To deal with tariff cuts across the board, rather than on an item-by-item basis; in effect, to remove the wall at once instead of a brick at a time.

5. To establish an adjustment assistance program for the relocation of industries and the training of workers and farmers adversely affected by tariff cuts. These adjustments included tax benefits, loans, and technical advice for firms or individuals affected by the tariff cuts. This feature replaced the peril-point provision and escape clauses of the old act which restricted tariff cuts if they caused injury to firms and workers. (This provision was made more flexible in the proposed Trade Act of 1970. See Chapter 18.)

It should be noted that the 1962 law was specifically pointed to the Common Market, even though the Market comprised only six of forty-four nations which then subscribed to the General Agreement on Tariffs and Trade (GATT) and conducted more than 80 percent of the world's trade. Thus the stage was set for the eventful five years which were to culminate in the Kennedy Round negotiations at Geneva in June 1967. The Kennedy Round will be discussed in the next chapter, but let us review some of the background of the law which made it possible and observe what happened to some of the hopes for economic integration.

UNFULFILLED DREAM

The dream of an Atlantic Community, European Partnership or the Grand Design of a Western World set against the Soviet-China bloc faded when France vetoed the first British application to the Common Market on British terms. Critics of the Trade Expansion Act of 1962, especially in Europe, argued that the Act was drawn on the assumption that Great Britain would become a member of the Common Market and the United States would continue its influence by sending products, especially agricultural products, into the Common Market countries under the low price import policies of Great Britain. Then France withdrew her forces from the integrated military establishment of NATO, making one more break in the solid military posture of the West against the East. All the nations of Western Europe, with varying degrees of timidity or aggressiveness, sought and established commercial relations with the Soviet Union and the Eastern European bloc in spite of strong pressure from the United States. The United States had consistently refused to liberalize trade restrictions against these countries, except in specific instances involving Yugoslavia and Poland.

The Eastern European bloc also has splintered. As a result of actions by Yugoslavia, then Poland, and now Romania, the economic strength of Eastern Europe is more myth than unity. While paying lip service to Soviet political ideology and following generally the Soviet foreign policy line in economic and trade matters, each country seems to interpret socialism for itself. Each is edging more toward the West in economics, trade, and culture; and there is a trend toward political and ideological neutrality.

With Great Britain denied admittance to the Common Market for a second time in 1966, with NATO and many of the devices designed to promote a solid Western European bloc against the East in considerable disarray, with a rising tendency in all Europe to "cease to be the tail on the great U.S. dog," and with only Great Britain willing to support the U.S. policy in South Vietnam, Europe—once again prosperous—cares little for "carrying the burden for the outside world" and prefers to live with communism rather than confront it by joining what appears to be a world crusade led by the United States. If another generation or a new world crisis provokes a new alignment, it will possibly be some form of Greater Europe, embracing some of the nations of Central Europe, rather than a tie with countries across the Atlantic.

The events of the past ten years have not only eroded the dream but have indefinitely delayed, if not eliminated, the formation of an Atlantic Community as an economic, political, and military bloc. The trend is away from geographical, political, or ideological arrangements and toward mutual economic accommodation between various countries of the Atlantic Community and Eastern Europe.

It is likely that the protective policies of the Six and the new Ten will continue to present serious problems for outside producers of temperate zone agricultural products. John O. Coppock in 1963 presented a masterly analysis of the thirteen countries which presumably would form the backbone of the Atlantic Community and the agricultural trade implications of such a union for the late 1950s. The two major surplus agricultural producers in the hypothetical Atlantic Community, the United States and Canada, produced temperate zone agricultural products at the annual rate of 72 million tons wheat equivalent. The agricultural deficit in the thirteen countries, which included Great Britain, was about 52 million tons. In other words, these thirteen countries imported 52 millions tons of temperate zone products. Even if

Canada and the United States had supplied all of this deficit—which they did not—a major surplus of 20 million tons would still have existed. Even with the deficit in the area remaining static and the production or surplus remaining static, it would take several years for population and consumption increase to balance out. Coppock forecast the necessity for rather extreme adjustment of production, which would probably have to come at the expense of the exporters, since the Common Agricultural Policy adopted by the Six would undoubtedly increase productivity in the EC area and Europe as a whole would move more toward self-sufficiency in temperate zone agricultural products rather than less.[1]

World events and divergent national policies have for the present taken European unity and political developments in other directions, and the problem of integrating agriculture into a larger Atlantic Community is not an issue. But the difficulties experienced by the Six in the past twelve years—coupled with mounting populations in other parts of the world—indicate quite clearly that the problem of those (individuals as well as countries) who have too much food and those who have too little remains one of the great basic issues confronting world leaders, diplomats, and humanitarians. An ideal solution will probably never come, but it is a problem that the nations of the earth will have to continue to try to solve. No alchemy of science or push-button gadgets have yet been developed to meet the basic problem of food, without which man cannot exist.

---

1. John O. Coppock, *North Atlantic Policy, The Agricultural Gap*, Twentieth Century Fund Study, 1963.

Chapter 8

The Kennedy Round

The Kennedy Round of negotiations under the General Agreement on Tariffs and Trade (GATT), which ended in midsummer 1967 and the results of which will come into full effect by 1972, was one of the most significant and far-reaching events concerning international trade in this century. It was not so much the amount of tariff reduction or even the increased trade implied by the agreement that was so important; rather, the significance was in the implications for international trade in the future.

As was anticipated during the preparations for the negotiations, agriculture was among the most troublesome issues to be resolved. There were several "firsts" in the negotiations:

For the first time agricultural issues were considered as part of the total package of negotiations. Previously, agricultural problems in trade negotiations had been segregated because of the many nontariff mechanisms various nations used to protect their domestic producers.

For the first time an American president, through his representatives at the negotiating table, could in effect "trade one concession for another"; that is, he could agree to U.S. reductions or not agree, depending on the cooperation of other countries.

For the first time the U.S. negotiator was responsible to both the executive department and the Congress of the United States.

And for the first time a bloc of nations, the European Community, negotiated as a single unit.

Thus the largest agricultural importing area of the world, the European Community, was placed in confrontation with the largest ag-

61

ricultural exporter in the world, the United States of America. When
Great Britain, the single largest importer of agricultural products in the
world, and Canada, the world's second largest agricultural exporter,
were brought into the picture, together with thirty-two other nations
—all with varied mechanisms for protecting their agricultural producers
—the complexity of the situation became apparent. That something
was accomplished is surely significant and offers hope that future negotiations will achieve some of the goals which, for a variety of reasons,
were left unrealized during the Kennedy Round.

BACKGROUND

To understand what happened to agricultural tariffs at Geneva in
1967, one must look back to the changes in American policy development in 1962 and the parallel evolution of the Common Agricultural
Policy in the Common Market. The Trade Expansion Act of 1962
was predicated on conditions which seemed likely to develop in Western
Europe and the Atlantic Community. First, the planners anticipated
that if Britain's pending membership in the Common Market were
accepted, her low price and import policies on agricultural products
would somehow dilute the highly protectionist systems of the six states
in the Community. Second, the planners nurtured at least the dream
that there would be an Atlantic Community to offset what was then
assumed to be a Soviet-dominated Eastern Europe. Finally, the planners
expected that when the Six agreed on basic principles of the Common
Agricultural Policy, specific price and support levels for EC agricultural
products would be determined quickly. None of these predictions became realities: Britain was not accepted in the Common Market, the
concept of an Atlantic Community went by the wayside, and the details of the Common Agricultural Policy were not resolved until the
last few hours of the Kennedy Round negotiations in 1967.

Early in 1962 each of the nations which agreed to negotiate new
agreements began making lists of products upon which they were willing
to negotiate tariff concessions. Then they turned to the important decision of how the negotiations would take place: item by item, the whole
list at once, industry in one category and agriculture in another (as in
the past) or simultaneously.

NEGOTIATIONS

The United States lost the battle with the Common Market on the
question of fixed tariffs vs. flexible levies. The United States preferred
to negotiate a lower fixed tariff on all products; the Common Agricultural Policy already had provided for flexible levies. Arguments over how

binding negotiations on agriculture could take place when the flexible levy system was involved resulted in months of wrangling and jockeying, to the considerable discomfort and impatience of the other partners. These arguments, however, illustrated seriously opposing views.

As an answer to the question of how to stabilize world agricultural prices under the Common Market variable levy system, Sicco Mansholt, Vice-President of the Common Market Commission, brought out the second Mansholt plan. It was essentially a variable levy system for the world, with the establishment of a world reference price for each farm commodity. The scheme would, in effect, set up a series of international agreements for each commodity, and a reference price for each commodity would be negotiated by the signatories of the agreement. In this arrangement members of the Common Market would be one of the signatories to the agreement similiar to the renewed International Wheat Agreement which emerged from the Kennedy Round negotiations. The scheme would bind the support any signatory would give its producers. The Kennedy Round approved an increase in the price of wheat. Specifically, the Mansholt plan would place the burden of adjusting supply on the exporting countries; thus it would not be necessary for the Common Market countries to reduce their incentives and adjust their production to allow for more imports of a given agricultural commodity from third countries (see Chapter 9 on operation of flexible levies).

The United States, as was to be expected, objected to this plan. Orville Freeman, then Secretary of Agriculture, criticized it as a move to "turn all import duties or other import barriers on agricultural products in all negotiations into variable levies of the kind applied in the Common Market countries." Offering an alternative approach, he advocated tying negotiations on agricultural items directly to industrial items. Under the Freeman plan a concession on industrial products in the United States would call for a compensatory concession on American agricultural products entering a particular country. Freeman also argued that the agricultural problem required different approaches, depending on whether the products were protected by fixed tariffs, target prices (those involving variable levies), or quotas or other regulations on quality or of a sanitary nature. For products on which there was a fixed tariff he suggested "binding" at a reasonable level; if no tariffs were involved (as in the case of cotton and soybeans from the United States) they would be bound free of duties. For other items he suggested a system of market sharing, that is, a guaranteed percentage of the total import. Freeman's market sharing idea was incorporated in the British grain agreement of 1963. The principal exporters of grain were guaranteed a percentage of British purchases based on their sales to Britain during the previous three-year period. Freeman would have liked for the European Community countries—as well as Great Britain, Japan, and other major importers of temperate zone products—to assure outside producers of a share in their domestic markets.

The Common Market countries finally ended the long debate they had been conducting among themselves on the future of internal support programs to improve or protect the income of producers in the Market countries. They agreed on the Hallstein Doctrine, named for Walter Hallstein of Germany, then chief executive officer of the Common Market Commission. According to the Hallstein Doctrine, "the programs of support granted to each agricultural product in each country should be bound at their present level and that within that margin all should be free to choose their own method of providing this support." This solution did not end the argument with the United States, and debate continued to the very last hours of the negotiations in 1967.

As early as the summer of 1965 British observers predicted that the negotiations would fail unless one side or the other—the United States or the Common Market—changed its position. These observers saw three choices for the United States: (1) to lower their sights (that is, abandon simultaneous industrial and agricultural negotiations with across-the-board percentage cuts), (2) to accept some sort of compromise in the hopes that future negotiations would correct the errors, or (3) to "blow up the Kennedy Round" (international trade agreements would remain about the same as they had been). As might be expected, the United States settled on a compromise of sorts.

When the hard-knuckle bargaining on 6,500 different industrial and agricultural items began in late 1966, four general goals had been agreed upon by all parties: (1) tariff reductions of 50 percent across the board—agricultural and industrial, (2) coverage of all classes of products, (3) accessibility of the products of all countries into world markets, (4) negotiations of both tariff and nontariff barriers restricting export of products of the less developed countries into the industrialized nations.

The industrial lists were rather quickly and generally agreed upon with two exceptions—chemicals imported into the United States and steel and aluminum tariff schedules. A stalemate soon developed on agriculture, partly because of the adamant position of the United States but mainly because of the Common Market's failure to arrive at a common basic price for grain. Negotiations went ahead on other issues such as access to the Common Market, support mechanisms, flexible levies, quotas, and nontariff protected items. Discussions on many livestock, dairy, and poultry products as well as many varieties of grain and oil crops could not be undertaken until a grain price policy was established.

To work out the details of possible tariff reductions and the mechanisms for making such tariff agreements effective, two major committees were established in 1965. One committee worked on grain prices and grain price policy; the other on meat, livestock, dairy, and poultry products. At the same time, other committees were working on lesser products such as fruits and vegetables; canned meat; all other types of canned food; dried beans, peas, and lentils; and a long list of minor

items extremely important to European countries but of little conse-
quence to the United States and other exporters of major agricultural
items.

The first change in the position taken by the United States was
abandonment of the principle of across-the-board tariff reductions; U.S.
negotiators agreed to selective cuts and accepted the flexible levy system
as applied in the Common Market countries. The committees working
on fruits and vegetables and other minor items came up with recommendations that were rather quickly accepted by all sides as workable
and acceptable, although these recommendations were less than the
goal of 50 percent across-the-board reductions. The committee on meat,
dairy, and poultry products, having met for days with no agreement in
sight, made no recommendations. Here U.S. policy negatively determined
the results. Just as the committee was about to arrive at methods for
increasing trade in these products, Congress and the White House decreased the quotas on Danish blue cheese and other dairy products. As a
result these products were deleted from the list of negotiable items and
left as they were, fully exposed to the flexible levy system of the Common Market. This means that European prices on these items may be
raised or lowered, the products let in or shut out of Europe completely
as the Commissioners in the European Community see fit.

The main battle was in the grain committee where the basic issue
was the price level of grain within the Six. The negotiations seemed to
dangle between total failure and collapse. The U.S. negotiators clashed
with Common Market spokesmen on both the principle and the implications of Article Three of the general guidelines—suitable conditions
for the access of products of all countries to the world market. The
United States and other exporting countries had held out for a percentage of the total imports of agricultural products into the Common
Market area, particularly on bread grain and feed grain. At the time,
the Common Market area claimed 90 percent self-sufficiency in agricultural products; the United States held out for a guaranteed portion of
such import market as existed in 1966 and an agreement, based on a
percentage of trade over the past three years, similar to the grain agreement with Great Britain. However, by now Great Britain had abandoned
the idea of a percentage guarantee and sided with the Common Market
in advocating very few guarantees, if any at all. The Common Market
negotiators offered a market-sharing arrangement which would cover 10
percent of the agricultural products imported by Market countries; the
United States held out for 15 percent.

GRAIN SURPLUS

In spite of the real need of many countries for food which they are
unable to buy on a commercial basis, there was in 1971 still an over-

supply of grain on the world market from a commercial standpoint. The United States is understandably concerned that other exporting countries have not accepted the responsibility of reducing production by their fair share. At the same time, the United States insists that Common Market countries reduce the incentives for their own producers to increase production, particularly of cereals. As far back as 1964 the United States and France insisted that domestic policies should be considered in establishing market access, tariff reductions, and quota restrictions. Although the Common Market agreed to this idea in principle, it was never a part of important decisions.

The grain negotiations of 1967 stalled as the result of two problems. The exporters insisted on guarantees that EC countries would continue to import from them not less than the volume imported in 1966. This would not impair the present relationships, but it would require the importing countries to adjust their production programs in order to absorb this amount of outside grain. The second difficult issue for negotiations on wheat tariffs was whether to increase the prices of wheat above those prevailing under the International Wheat Agreement. In the end the exporters abandoned the idea of guaranteed access, but they won an increase in the floor prices for wheat. The International Wheat Agreement then in effect required importers to pay a base price of $1.50 per bushel for Manitoba No. 1 at Canadian and Gulf ports.[1] The Agreement did not cover floor prices for certain kinds of soft wheat (No. 1 and No. 2) and other finer points in the grain trade. In an attempt to reach a new agreement, American base price for No. 1 wheat was set at $1.73 per bushel in Gulf ports. Once this item had been agreed upon, the issues which had been neglected in the old agreement were speedily resolved. The action came after the United States compromised by lowering tariffs on imported chemicals.

GOALS VERSUS RESULTS

Now that more than four years have passed since the negotiations and the ratification of the grain agreement by the United States, one may attempt some comparison of the results with the goals set out in the beginning. Limited achievement does not obscure the fact that negotiations in the Kennedy Round were the most far reaching, covered the largest number of items, and made the most significant selective cuts in tariffs of any of the international negotiations under GATT.

The United States was forced to abandon insistence on a guaranteed portion of Common Market imports. No agreement was attained on: feed grains and other products used for livestock and poultry feed; dairy products, meat, poultry, or sugar; the nontariff barriers to international

---

1. The International Wheat Agreement expired June 30, 1971, and was not renewed.

agricultural trade—that is, quotas, internal taxes, quality, and detailed packaging and sanitary regulations; the mechanics of policing or co-ordinating internal domestic policies.

The original goal of an international code for agricultural trade was abandoned. The most important achievement was an international agreement which set meaningful gate or reference prices for the Common Market and established a schedule of differentials on various grades and qualities which made workable the so-called floor prices. Collateral agreements set up an antidumping code which required a "fair and open procedure in measures for export promotion."

The nations concerned agreed to a $4.5 billion food aid program whereby those countries with surplus food would share it with needy nations. Members of the European Community having no surplus food were to make contributions in cash. The United States is a major bene-ficiary of the food aid program, not only because it lessens the burden on the limited supply of some commodities but also because some of the cash contributions will be spent for food, particularly in the United States. The program calls for the United States to contribute 42 percent of the $4.5 billion in wheat and cash, for Common Market contributions of 23 percent, for Canada 10 percent, United Kingdom 5 percent, Japan 5 percent, Switzerland 0.7 percent, Argentina 0.5 percent; 12 percent was left for non-GATT members of the International Wheat Agreement to assume.

Substantial tariff cuts were made and some trade limitations were removed on the so-called nonbasic items. Nonbasic items, while relatively insignificant in total world trade, are very important to groups and areas in the United States. The agreement on agriculture, so far as the United States was concerned, was disappointing. However, U.S. negotiators took heart in the fact that there were no losses on so-called "bound ar-rangements." These involved principally soybeans and cotton and other fibers which had been entering the European markets without tariffs. A strong effort had been made by the Common Market group to make them subject to the variable levy system.

In round numbers the United States made concessions on $8.5 bil-lion worth of imports. Actual tariff reductions were granted on $7.9 billion dollars worth of the total. Existing rates were "bound" on $150 million worth, and $400 million worth of imports were admitted duty free. Countries which exported to the United States made concessions of $30 billion worth of products, of which $7.7 billion were to the United States. Common Market countries annually imported $836 million worth of minor items—fruits, vegetables, canned goods, dried beans and lentils—about 10 percent of which came from the United States. Tariff reduc-tions on these items ranged from 1 percent to 50 percent. The Com-mon Market reduced tariffs on products from third countries which had previously been valued at $130 million, about $20 million of which rep-resented U.S. products. The Common Market countries agreed to tariff reductions of more than 50 percent on products constituting $3 million of the U.S. portion of this trade, a 50 percent reduction on products valued at $12 million, a cut of 25–49 percent on goods worth $1.7 million, and reductions of less than 25 percent on the remainder. All items considered, thirty-two countries made tariff concessions on $900 million worth of agricultural products which they imported from the United States—especially canned and fresh fruits and vegetables, soybeans and other oilseeds, cotton, tobacco, tallow, certain canned meats, and dairy products. On the other side, the United States made tariff concessions on $700 million worth of agricultural imports, most noticeably on tropical items such as jute, coffee, coconuts, pineapples, and other commodities not directly competitive with U.S. agricultural products.

Undoubtedly trade will expand in many sectors when all of the agreements stemming from the Kennedy Round go into effect. However, it is also evident that, except in rare cases, further tariff reductions will have little or no effect on the volume of trade. In the future, negotiators will have to consider nontariff barriers to trade if they are to make additional progress. They will need to deal with the difficult problems of quotas, internal taxes, and the flexible levy system of the Common Market countries—probably the most effective device yet developed for protecting internal prices.

When asked why the Common Market group maintained such a rigid stand on flexible levies and other devices for the protection of agricultural industries, a spokesman for the Common Market countries pointed out that one of the basic objectives of the Common Agricultural Policy was to improve the income and well-being of the rural population. How else could this be done over the short period? He also noted that the negotiations had come at a time when the Common Market group was giving far more attention to its internal stresses and problems than to the outside world. He further stated that the Common Market countries were confident that the United States saw the Common Market as more promising for the sale of industrial goods than for agricultural products, and that U.S. industrialists would not let the negotiations fail even if a mere face-saving device were the only alternative for the agricultural group. Moreover, as it turned out, the U.S. negotiators did not sacrifice agriculture for the sake of industry or betray the instructions President Lyndon B. Johnson issued, "that the United States will enter into no ultimate agreement unless progress is registered toward trade liberalization in products of our farms as well as our factories."

Admittedly, U.S. agricultural interests did not achieve all they had hoped for. Still, the United States stood by its position that something had to be accomplished in the agricultural trade area. Progress was made.

Chapter 9

OPERATION OF THE COMMON MARKET

IN THE YEARS since the Rome Treaty of 1957, the institutional structure and machinery for operating the Common Market have shown remarkable capacity and resilience. The treaty provided four institutions, patterned after those of the European Coal and Steel Community structure, to manage the intricate task of economically integrating the six nations of the Common Market: (1) the Parliament or Assembly, (2) the Council of Ministers, (3) the Court of Justice, and (4) the Commission. There are also various subordinate committees and subcommittees.

The Assembly is the Parliament or Congress of the Common Market and also serves the European Atomic Energy Community (Euratom) and the European Coal and Steel Community (ECSC). Delegates are named from each country by their respective parliaments and represent national interests. Due to France's opposition to a supergovernment, the Assembly has not been especially active.

The Council of Ministers, with headquarters in Brussels, serves the legislative function in the Common Market structure. The principal duties of the Council of Ministers are to coordinate the policies of the member states, formulate general policy, and make the decisions required to carry out the mandates of the treaty. France, Germany, and Italy have two votes each in the Council; Belgium, Luxembourg, and the Netherlands each have one vote. The Rome Treaty required that decisions of the Council be unanimous during the first two years and after that by majority vote. Common practice is still to act only by unanimous vote on all basic issues. The membership of the Council is national and represents each nation's interests. However, it may not have the same persons for each meeting or session. For instance, if the main subject to be acted upon is agriculture, the Council for that particular meeting may be representatives from each country familiar with the agricultural problem. The Assembly, the Court of Justice, and the Council of Ministers have equal status in the organizational scheme of the Common Market and, except for the Court, represent national interests.

The Court of Justice, consisting of seven judges and two advocate generals (two each from France, Germany, and Italy and one each from Belgium, Luxembourg, and the Netherlands), is independent of national interests. The Court insures adherence to the provisions of the Rome Treaty, hears cases brought by individuals and organizations, and reviews the legality of Council and Commission decisions.

The Commission is the executive branch, the nerve center of the Common Market operations. In most cases the Commission has sole power to initiate action. It is composed of nine members named by common agreement among the member states: two each from France, Italy, and Germany and one each from Belgium, Luxembourg, and the Netherlands. Unlike the delegates to the Council and the Assembly who speak for national interests, the Commissioners are international servants who speak for the Common Market as a whole. The functions are to supervise the application of the treaty, to recommend programs to the Council of Ministers, and to execute and carry out the day-to-day operations of the Common Market. Management committees operate below the Commission, making studies and recommendations and supplying the expertise for operations. As an example, the Commission's responsibilities include recommendations for import levies on poultry products, grain, oilseeds, or other agricultural items. The Council of Ministers makes the final decision on amount of the levy. However, the Commission may decide to fix the levies for three-month periods rather than annually. When the Commission makes such a decision, it may go to the Management Committee on poultry for advice and consultation. If that committee agrees by majority vote, the order goes out; if it disagrees, the order goes back to the Council which can overrule the committee's adverse recommendation. When the Commission makes a recommendation to the Council, it sends it at the same time to the Permanent Representatives of the member states. These are in effect watchdogs stationed permanently at Brussels. They represent national interests, and it is their duty to keep Council members fully informed on the implications of a particular order to the home industry.

This structure sounds unwieldy and bureaucratic. However, it has proved to be remarkably effective and exceedingly flexible, especially in protecting the interests of the member states. It has been effective in resolving many of the conflicts which are bound to arise in attempts to integrate six vastly different and varied systems of agriculture. The Common Agricultural Policy, outlined in 1958, looked toward the integration of all phases of management of the six agricultural economies by 1970. However, in 1962 the date for completion of integration was set for June 30, 1968. Between 1958 and 1968 common prices and procedures to enforce price decisions did come into being for more than 90 percent of Common Market agricultural production, and common external tariffs were established. Still to be achieved by December 31, 1968, the end of the transition period, were agreement on border taxes, a common approach to nontariff barriers, common sanitary and health regulations, a common table of tolerances for herbicides on imported food products, and a whole series of small but important regulations which remained the responsibility of the national governments. These issues are still under Committee study.

FUNDAMENTAL ISSUES

A number of more fundamental issues in the agricultural sector must be settled if complete integration of the economies is to be achieved. Most important of these to world agricultural interests is a common commercial trade policy with outside countries.[1] There is a common tariff policy, but there has been no common external trade policy. Each nation has more or less made its trade arrangements according to its own interests, with approval of the Commission. Normally, approval is given automatically. However, during the last years of the transition period, some steps were taken to adopt a common trade policy in making trade agreements with outside countries. An antidumping regulation was adopted in 1968; common rules for agricultural and industrial imports from nonmember countries (excluding the Communist bloc) were agreed to; bilateral trade accords will be permitted on an exceptional basis until January 1, 1973.

Now that the transition period has ended, these arrangements must be formally approved by the Council of Ministers. Also initiation of special trade arrangements with third countries must come from the Commission rather than from individual countries. In practice one country still initiates the action, or, as in the case of Yugoslavia, the outside country initiates it and the Commission and Council act on the application.

SPECIAL ARRANGEMENTS

A few purely commercial trade agreements have been made between the Six and outside countries. The first such agreement was

---

1. On January 1, 1970, a common foreign trade policy was put into effect for most countries outside the Soviet bloc. A common worldwide trade policy is to become effective January 1, 1973. After that date all trade negotiations will be conducted by the enlarged Common Market.

arranged in December 1963 with Iran. Since the Iranian agreement is
fairly typical of one of the four ways by which an outside country may
be given trade preferences with the Six, it is worth examining in some
detail. Iran traditionally has been a good market for industrial products
of Common Market countries. At the same time, Iranian oil and agricultural crops have found markets in the Common Market countries. It
seemed advantageous to work out some arrangement which would allow
Iranian products some preference in the Market countries. Iranian
carpets, dried fruit, and caviar were subject to varying tariff levels in
each of the Community countries. The agreement that materialized
left tariffs at a high level but provided for a 90 percent cut in the carpet
tariff, a 1 percent cut on raisins and dried apricots, and a 6 percent reduction on caviar. The agreement called for an eventual common tariff
on Iranian products of about 8 percent. Some Iranian agricultural
products negotiated in the Kennedy Round come under the present external tariff system which, among other things, provides for no tariff on
cotton—an important Iranian export to Italy. The Iranian agreement
of 1963 was to last three years, and it has been renewed for items not
covered in the Kennedy Round.

ASSOCIATE STATES

Another issue standing in the way of complete integration involves
the associate states. Some eighteen former French, Dutch, and Italian
colonies have made limited preference arrangements with the Common
Market. Many countries of Africa and Asia now seek such arrangements.
There was some sentiment in the EC to abandon special preferences for
developing countries, leaving the whole issue of preferences for developing countries to the United Nations Conference on Trade and Development (UNCTAD). However, these preference agreements were renewed
in late 1969.

BILATERAL TRADE RULES

Presently trade between the Common Market and the nations of
Western and Eastern Europe is increasing, and each member of the
Six makes its own bilateral arrangements with the country involved.
For example, Germany may wish to sell industrial products in Poland,
while Poland wishes to sell cattle or some other agricultural product in
Germany. A bilateral agreement is signed and then approved by the
Common Market's Council of Ministers. Similar procedures are fol-
lowed with nations of Western Europe and Africa. Austria and Switzer-
land are not members of the EC but are associated with the European
Free Trade Association (EFTA). Austria gets a special preference
arrangement for timber shipped to Germany—her principal customer.

Switzerland, with 45 percent of her trade with the EC, does not have preference arrangements; but much of her export is covered by the General Agreement on Tariffs and Trade (GATT), and she competes in that market on an equal basis with other outside countries. The individual countries of EFTA have dealt with the Market individually rather than as a trade bloc, as was anticipated when EFTA was established.

Making these bilateral agreements is not as simple and non-controversial as may appear. Denmark traditionally has exported surplus cattle to Western Germany, which in recent years has admitted a quota of 200,000 head annually. Presently Germany is seeking to expand trade with the East; and the cattle raisers of Poland, Hungary, Yugoslavia, and other Eastern European countries are interested in selling in West Germany. In the summer of 1968 the Community boosted levies on imported cattle so high that they virtually eliminated trade with Denmark. As expected, Denmark protested bitterly, and Germany responded with an application for an import quota of an additional 15,000 head—under special preference—in order to buy Danish cattle. The German request was approved within hours by the Council. When asked why Germany did not ask special preference for Denmark for the old quota of 200,000 head, a German official replied that Germany had other friends and potential customers who wanted to sell cattle into Germany and that it was in Germany's interest to spread the quota around.

CONTROLS

The Common Agricultural Policy on beef and beef products (the area is deficit in these items) is designed to encourage domestic producers to increase their production and to protect consumers against high beef prices. The system for unifying beef and cattle prices and encouraging production within the Six went into effect in November 1964. The objectives were to be obtained through support prices, purchases, and levies in intracountry and third-country trade. Since inedible tallow, hides, skins, and beef casings were not listed in the common regulations, the main livestock-derived exports from the United States were not affected. Edible tallow and beef variety meats were included in the EC regulations, but tariffs on edible tallow had been bound under GATT at 2 percent and on beef variety meats at 20 percent. (The Kennedy Round reduced the tallow tariff from 2 to 1 percent ad valorem.)

Imports of beef and cattle are controlled in three ways: by the Common Market's variable levies, by quotas, and by import certificates. The variable levies on live cattle and dressed beef and veal are applicable only when prices in the Common Market fall below a specified level. This is the main device for maintaining prices that are neither too high for the consumer nor too low for the producer. Each year the Market countries establish a target or gate price in each member state. Gate prices are established for other farm products under Common Market control. This target price represents what the country feels would be a desirable wholesale price somewhere between 93 and 96 percent of the target or going price. This is the so-called intervention price. Whenever the average market price for cattle falls below the intervention price for seven successive days, the government may purchase cattle until the market price rises above that level. Further, when the price rises 5 percent or more above the intervention price, no levies may be imposed on imports. Since beef is one of the few deficit items of Common Market agriculture, this particular arrangement has been highly useful from the internal market standpoint. Its operation, however (as illustrated by the case of West Germany and Denmark), has caused concern by third countries seeking outlets for beef.

Other items under Market control—butter and poultry—have not been handled so successfully. Butter surpluses have been piling up in the Market area for several years and now exceed 300,000 tons. Poultry, while not subject to government purchase, has been protected by increasingly high levies and is being exported to third-country markets under subsidies provided in the Guarantee Fund. Subsidies to make Common Market products competitive in world markets are limited, however. The Commission recommends and the Council approves a general level of subsidy for a given category of trade, and the subsidies are usually held within this limit. Under special conditions a member state may request and receive the approval of the Commission for an increased subsidy in order to make a deal. This happened in the summer of 1968 when France, by requesting an extra subsidy, underbid the United States in a large purchase of barley by Japan.

The principles of target prices, import levies, and intervention prices are generally followed in grain and other agricultural products as they are in the beef and cattle trade. Fruits and vegetables are the exception (see Chapter 3). Under the Common Agricultural Policy, prices of feed grain, meat, dairy products, and poultry products are based on the price of bread grain, therefore, the management of bread grain prices and trade is of vital concern. The International Wheat Agreement somewhat stabilized the world price level of wheat and the trade relations between the Six and third countries. However, provisions in the agreement which concern various grades of wheat and the use of wheat for feed have created problems and resulted in less price stability than originally anticipated. These troublesome provisions were the subject of considerable discussion by members of the International Grains Agreement meeting in Washington in the spring of 1969. At the time there was some prospect of breaking up the agreement.[2] The In-

---

2. The member states of the International Wheat Agreement were unable to agree on a price system, and the agreement was not renewed when the original agreement expired in 1970.

ternational Wheat Agreement to some extent regularizes and establishes rules for international grain trade. The management of grains within the Common Market is an internal matter similar to that in any outside country. The management of grains internally not only affects the economies of each of the Six but has a strong impact on exporting countries.

On August 1 each year the Agricultural Commission submits to the Council a schedule of prices for various cereals such as wheat, meslin, rye, barley, oats, maize, buckwheat, millet, canary seed, and grain sorghum and a series of processed products such as meal, flour, and groats. These are guaranteed prices and are to be effective for the following season. They are, in effect, support prices; the system is similar to that used in the United States and Eastern European countries. The guaranteed prices are usually higher than world prices and are also the reference prices against which subsidies are paid when such products are exported. Levies on imports are usually high enough to make the prices of imported products higher than the minimum support prices for EC products. The levies may be raised or lowered at will under the procedures described earlier in this chapter. This is probably the most obnoxious feature of the levy system, since it permits no long-range planning on the part of exporting countries. As an example, the basic support price for soft wheat in the summer of 1968 was $98.75 per ton. If supply and demand within the Common Market caused the market to fall, the farmer would sell to the government for $98.75 per ton. At the same time the reference or gate price for wheat was established at $104 plus per ton. The world price—the price at which the United States desired to sell to Common Market members—was $65 per ton CIF Rotterdam. The levy then would be the difference between these figures—about $39 per ton.

Receipts from levies are paid into the Guarantee Fund, from which the EC supports prices of other agricultural commodities, pays for programs to bring structural change in agriculture, and subsidizes exports. In the case of exports, the Council fixes the amount of subsidy for each commodity. As mentioned above, this subsidy may be increased under special rules. Exporters in the Common Market sell against the world price, and the Guarantee Fund pays the difference between what they actually receive and the guaranteed minimum price. This system has been criticized by some of the member countries, who argue that some commercial firms are taking advantage of the system and collecting enormous sums in the mere process of trading. In other words, the Market imports 10 million tons of outside wheat and collects levies on it, and exports about 10 million tons of its own wheat and pays an export subsidy on it. This system is defended by the differentials for location which make it more profitable, for example, to import wheat for certain consuming areas than to move it from the European production area to the consuming market. Further, the imported wheat is usually of a special quality such as durum (not widely grown in Europe), hard winter, or varieties needed for blending purposes. No one seems to know at this point how much of the wheat trade is created for purposes of manipulation and how much is based on actual need.

The same subsidy and levy system operates to some extent with cheese production. An Eastern European country may produce certain specialty cheese demanded by a sector of the Common Market consumers. The cheese is imported by a Common Market country (presently under bilateral arrangements) subject to the variable levy system. In turn, the importing country sells quantities of its own cheese either to the exporting country or some other outside country and collects the export subsidy on it.

Intervention levies may be imposed if the levy provided in the annual price support and levy scale is threatened by price breaks in the world market. However, intervention levies are not used on all products. In the case of meat and dairy products, only butter is subject to intervention levies. Poultry, eggs, and pork are subject to what are called supplemental levies, which are also used to offset the difference in cost of feed grains produced in third countries and those produced in the Community. This supplementary levy affords the Community producer full cost of production protection.

Sugar is an important import and export item in all countries of the Six. The sugar trade is regulated partially by the International Sugar Agreement and partially by a series of internal production quotas. There are no quotas on imports and exports. Management of sugar production is designed primarily to protect internal sugar prices; thus there are special support programs in Italy and Germany to offset the relatively high cost of production in these countries. Each grower of sugarbeets in the Community receives a production quota, and a grower receives the full support price for the sugar if he produces no more than 135 percent of his quota. If he exceeds 135 percent, he receives no support.

In the case of poultry, Common Market prices supposedly are maintained through the use of regular and intervention levies which represent 18 cents per pound more than the actual prices received by the producers in the United States. The producers of surplus poultry in the Six (principally West Germany and Holland) battle in the marketplaces of third-country markets and have depressed the entire world price for poultry products. With poultry products booming within the Six under the protective levy system, the annual establishment of regular and intervention prices becomes a statistical game, the object of which is to find a compromise that will satisfy the small producers as well as the large mass-production installations. Such prices are arrived at by converting pounds of feed grain into one pound of meat. The conversion ratio adopted as a pricing base is therefore of major concern. If the minimum is set against the conversion ratio of three pounds of feed for one pound of meat (a relatively high minimum price), when the world prices fall below that, levies—both regular and intervention—go into force. In other words, the higher the gate price, the sooner intervention levies take hold. The conversion ratio of poultry meat to a pound of feed is 2.4 in Holland and in the United States about 2.3.

The Danes, who export about 80 percent of their poultry production, have instituted a two-price system in their poultry, pork, and egg industries.[3] They levied a domestic sales tax on poultry and pork products (which they distributed among producers) and cut export prices. The Community responded by imposing a supplemental levy. The Danes countered by increasing the margin between their domestic and export prices. The export price of Danish poultry is now about 24 cents per pound, compared to a gate or reference price of 32 cents per pound for poultry coming into the Community. This has drastically reduced Danish sales to Germany. The high export payments by the Six on poultry products (now 13 cents per pound) make Common Market products highly competitive with Danish and U.S. products in third-country markets such as Austria, Switzerland, and Greece. Before the system was initiated, the United States had 66 percent of the Swiss market. It fell to less than 3.7 percent, but some has been regained by U.S. heavy subsidies.

Successes and Problems

It is evident that the system, while effective for the Common Market countries, presents serious problems for outside countries. The Common Market has succeeded in protecting its internal price structure, in raising the income of Community producers, and in reaching near self-sufficiency in practically every agricultural products of the temperate zone except beef. In the process of this achievement, it has created new problems within the Community and aroused grave concern in the United States and other countries. The burdensome surplus of butter and the high cost of subsidizing poultry and soft wheat exports, for example, are new problems which have caused the Community to seek immediate ways and means of cutting this cost and reducing the surplus. In the case of wheat, farmers are now being paid heavy subsidies to use locally produced denatured wheat for feed grain, thus cutting down the imports of feed grains from the United States and other exporting countries. The mountains of butter call for efforts to increase consumption of butter and reduce consumption of margarine. This effort may well affect the $500 million export business the United States annually enjoys in soybeans and soybean products. In order to discourage the use of margarine by making it higher in cost and more comparable in price with butter, a $60 per ton tax has been proposed on soybeans going into

3. When the transition period for Danish membership in the Common Market ends in 1977, these devices for price support will be eliminated.

the Common Market. In order to discourage purchases of oilseed cake for feed and possibly encourage more wheat and rye conversion to feed grain, a $30 per ton tax on oilseed cake has been proposed. The object is to cut production of surplus items by increasing production costs. The United States has strongly opposed these schemes. There is yet no final decision.

The United States will seek to change Common Market practices detrimental to U.S. exporters through negotiation. Failing this, the United States may choose to meet the competition by increasing subsidies to U.S. exporters or by retaliating through international channels. In one instance the United States has already chosen increased subsidies. This resulted in the so-called poultry war (see Chapter 4). The cost in 1969 of the subsidy to poultry exporters was about $3.7 million—more than the U.S. producer received for his poultry in the first instance. The same type of situation developed in the case of lard exports to Great Britain. Lard exported by the Common Market to Great Britain under large subsidies virtually wiped out the U.S. market there. In 1969 the United States began subsidizing lard exports to Great Britain, with the result that some of this market is being regained. These experiments in poultry and lard raise serious questions about U.S. agricultural trade policy. Eventually U.S. producers and the government will have to decide whether to plan agricultural operations on domestic needs and an unpredictable world market and live with the situation or to open a trade war of major proportions. For the present, the policy appears to be to try to work with the system. It is probably better to sacrifice a few million dollars worth of poultry exports in order to compete in the world market with feed grains and oilseeds and other products needed by Europe to produce poultry and wheat products.

Chapter 10

FUNDING THE COMMON MARKET POLICY

☙

THE EUROPEAN COMMUNITY has three financial instruments with which to carry out the objectives of the Common Agricultural Policy—the European Development Fund, the European Investment Bank, and the Guarantee and Guidance Fund. Each of these institutions was provided for in the Treaty of Rome. The European Development Fund, mainly concerned with associate states, was further formalized in the Yaounde Convention held in the Cameroon Republic in 1963. This meeting set up the Association Convention composed of eighteen African and Malagasy states (the association states) and the Common Market. The Convention agreement provided for reduction of trade barriers among the associate members and between the Common Market and the associate states. It also embodied an extensive program for diversifying the economies of the associate states and for integrating the agricultural development of these areas with the Common Market. The Convention ran for a period of five years and was renewed in 1969 for another five years.

EUROPEAN DEVELOPMENT FUND

The Association and the European Development Fund were provided for in Article 131 in the Treaty of Rome: "The purpose of this association shall be to promote the economic and social development of the overseas countries and territories . . . the association shall in the first place permit the furthering of interests and prosperity of the in-

habitants of these countries and territories in such a manner as to lead
them to the economic, social, and cultural development they expect."

The Development Fund receives its money from the governments of
the Six, with West Germany and France providing 34 and 35 percent
of the total respectively. For five years 30 percent of the fund was ear-
marked for social and cultural development (principally education and
health services) and the remaining 70 percent for the development of
infrastructure (roads, dams, public buildings, rivers, and harbors). The
Yaounde Convention committed the Development Fund to aid the associate states in integrating their economies and in diversifying and developing their total growth in such a way as to complement each other
and the Six. Other countries and territories related to the Six by
former colonial connections (Surinam, New Caledonia, French Somali-
land, Guiana, and Guadeloupe) have been assisted in various ways by
the Development Fund. With the end of the five-year test period, 1958–
63, the nature of the projects and the amounts of money allocated
changed considerably, due largely to the pressure of the African countries
for projects of interest to their own peoples. It was also necessary to
train and educate managers and personnel to operate and support some
of the infrastructure, either built or under way. Since projects and re-
quests for assistance must originate in the country or territory, the projects
were often poorly planned and improperly drawn. This required assignment by the fund of technicians to assist in planning and executing the
projects once they were approved. Delays between the conception and
advertising of the project and the time of visible results was a perplexing
element. The assignment of technicians to see projects through has
solved this problem to some extent. The average period between the
submission of a project to the Development Fund Commission and a
decision by the Commission on funding ranges from three months to
two years; from the decision by the Commission to the beginning of
work, from four to ten months.

Allocations of funds by the member countries to the Development
Fund are calculated in "units of account," each unit being the equivalent
of one U.S. dollar. The five-year program in 1963 called for expenditures of some 800 million units of account, or $800 million—roughly
$150 million per year. The test period provided for grants only. The
present program under the Yaounde Convention provides for grants,
special loans, and loans from the European Investment Bank which here-
tofore loaned only on projects in the European Community. Funds for
the five-year program ending in 1969 were divided as follows: outright
grants from the European Development Fund to the eighteen associate
states, $680 million; grants to overseas territories and countries not
associated with the Common Market, $60 million; special loans from the
fund to independent states, $46 million; and $4 million in loans to overseas territories. The European Investment Bank made normal loans
in the amount of $64 million to the independent states and $6 million

in loans to the overseas territories. This activity makes the European Community the world's fourth largest contributor of public funds to development on a per capita basis.

For what kind of projects are these funds allocated? The Convention provided that 25 percent of the total fund should be used for the diversification of the national economies based principally on one agricultural crop. There appears to be a project of some kind in marketing, land development, irrigation, and new crop research in each country designed to do just that. Other funds are used to expand production or improve marketing of tea, food crops, and improved cattle; to expand veterinary services; and to build processing plants. A glance over the 395 projects at the beginning of 1969 revealed over 200 projects of a social nature: 43 hospitals, 47 maternity and child care clinics, 157 field dispensaries, 4 research institutes, and several public health centers. In education the fund aided 17 colleges and secondary schools, 2,270 special primary classes, 6 teacher-training establishments, and the construction of more than 2,000 dwellings and classroom facilities with a wide variety of special training institutes for native teachers and leaders. In the area of rural modernization, there were projects for improved irrigation for cattle raising; new agricultural institutes for second, third, and lower level workers; village wells; 104 small irrigation dams; special training for 5,000 students in their home countries; and more than 1,000 scholarships for study abroad. Other areas of activity included asphalt roads in the Republic of the Congo, town planning in the Republic of Chad, research in tea growing and plantation management in Burundi, bridges and road surveys in Mali, new rights-of-way and new equipment for the principal railroad on Togo and electrification of the wharfs, and port extensions and modernization in Malagasy. The Development Fund employs 200 agents in twenty-nine associated countries and territories to control and watch over the work. These are but a few of the activities of the Development Fund, which now appears to be a permanent fixture of the European Community. Two significant developments are emerging. One is a new agriculture in the associate nations, complementary to the economies of the Six, and the other is the expectation that these states now in limited association with the Market will achieve full member status some time in the future.

Preferences granted to the products of the associate states are limited at present to a relatively few basic items, although the stated objective is free movement of all products between each state and the Community. The associate states agree to give tariff preference and to abolish quotas on European Community industrial products. As examples, coffee from the associate states enjoys a preference tariff of 9.6 percent against a tariff of 16 percent on coffee from outside states, cocoa runs 5.4 against 9 percent, fresh pineapples 9 against 12 percent, cloves 15 against 20 percent, coconut 4 against 5 percent, nutmeg 15 against

20 percent, pepper 17 against 20 percent, vanilla 11 against 15 percent, and tea 10 against 10 percent.

Two of the common criticisms of U.S. aid and economic development programs are: too often money is wasted on prestige projects, and money is misappropriated by local officials. According to officials who manage the fund, the European Development Fund has largely avoided these pitfalls. They cite three reasons:

1. The fund is administered by the Executive Commission of the Six with the assistance of a committee from the "Joint Council of the Association." This gives the Executive Commission not only power to prevent "prestige projects" but wide authority to direct the money to the kind of projects that will contribute to the diversification and integration of the economies of the eighteen associate states.

2. Once a project is accepted by the Commission, the local government calls for bids. Commission officials see that the bids are genuine, and they reserve the right to disapprove the contract. Payments are made by the Commission directly to the contractor as the work progresses. No project money goes into the local government's budget or treasury.

3. Local governments are responsible for the supervision of the contract, but technicians and engineers of the Commission staff double-check the work.

The fund is international and, according to officials, little playing of one state against another in order to gain extra favors has been indulged in. Materials used in the projects by the contractors are presumably purchased wherever the terms and conditions are most favorable. West Germany, however, contributor of 35 percent of the money in the Development Fund, protested in 1966 that only 8 percent of the total expenditures to that date had been spent in Germany.

EUROPEAN INVESTMENT BANK

Funds for the European Investment Bank consist of formal contributions by the member states. Until recently most loans were made to members of the Six for special development projects in agriculture. However, as noted earlier in this chapter, loans are now being made for projects in the associate member states. Greece received a commitment for a development loan of $125 million at the time of her application for membership in the Common Market in 1962 and a loan in 1967 of some $57 million for economic development of Crete.

GUARANTEE AND GUIDANCE FUND

The main instrument for providing stability and support for agriculture and for financing the structural changes deemed necessary in some of the Common Market countries is the Guarantee and Guidance Fund. Specifically this fund is charged with aiding structural improvement in agriculture, reducing surpluses by subsidizing exports to third countries, and intervening in local markets by purchase when the price of products falls below the support level (see Chapter 10). The money involved in the fund has grown from $20 million in 1963 to more than $800 million in 1970. The money is contributed by the member states in accordance with a scale fixed in the Rome Treaty. The original fund was made up by direct budget contributions from the member states under a formula: Italy 28 percent, Germany 28 percent, France 28 percent, the Netherlands 7.9 percent, and Belgium and Luxembourg 7.9 percent. After 1963–64 additional contributions were made in proportion to net imports of each member state. These amounted to only about 10 percent of the total expenditures in 1963–64, but by 1964–65, 20 percent of the funds came from the net import formula. Export refunds (subsidizing of exports) accounted for nearly 85 percent of all expenditures, with market intervention (maintaining minimum prices) accounting for the remainder. Very little of the fund in this period was spent for guidance or improvement of the structure of agriculture, although the amount allocated for the purpose has shown a steady increase. Market support purchases and export refunds dealing with grain, pork, eggs, poultry, milk products, rice, and olive oil totaled $259 million by 1965. In 1966 the breakdown by percentages on money spent on each product was as follows: 67.5 percent on grain price support and export and 26.1 percent on milk product operations; rice, pork, eggs, poultry, beef, and veal accounted for the remaining expenditures. By the end of 1969 the Guarantee Fund expenditures reached $800 million and and by 1971 more than $1 billion.

Beginning July 1, 1968, and ending December 31, 1969, contributions to the Guarantee and Guidance Fund by member states consisted of two components: 90 percent of the funds levied and collected by each member state on imports from nonmember countries, and funds contributed by member nations according to a fixed scale. This scale required Germany to contribute 31.2 percent of whatever had to be made up from the shortfall on levies, France 32 percent, Italy 20.3 percent, the Netherlands 8.2 percent, Belgium 8.1 percent, and Luxembourg 0.2 percent. After 1970 all receipts from levies, rather than 90 percent, were paid by each state into the fund.[1] Until July 1, 1968, the Guarantee Fund covered only part of the costs of market support and export subsidies, but thereafter it paid 100 percent of the costs of stabilizing the markets. In past years the fund has been a retroactive refunding agency; that is, it has reimbursed the members for a portion of their expenses in storage, market support, and export subsidies—usually about three years after the

1. Under the formula agreed upon for the entry of the United Kingdom to the Market, after 1973 the Guarantee and Guidance Fund will be supported by 100 percent of the import levies, the value-added tax, and all customs duties on all goods imported into the new enlarged area.

fact. Beginning in 1970 the fund became a permanent feature of the market operation and an automatic clearinghouse for current operations. As the guidance section of the fund has operated in the past, a member state seeking to improve its marketing system or to develop a particular phase of production or processing might ask for an advance to finance the changes. In 1967 Italy received an advance of $45 million for improvements in the marketing of olives, olive oil, fruits, and vegetables; Belgium received a smaller advance for its sugar marketing operations. A statement of account and expenditures on these and similar operations was made on December 31, 1969.

There were ten programs in various stages of operation in the three-year period 1967–69. The following guidelines governed the allocation of funds and the selection of programs:

1. The need to achieve a balance between programs concerning the pattern of production and those relating to structure and marketing.

2. The importance of each program for the implementation of the Common Market policy.

3. The opportunities for financing and carrying out the various types of operations in member countries (each country receiving assistance from the fund must pay at least 30 percent of the cost from its own budget).

The programs that emerged under these guidelines were in three categories. The first was programs to reduce unit costs and increase labor productivity. These included land reform, irrigation, drainage and forestry, and operations to improve farm structures. The second category was programs to achieve optimum prices for farm products. This included projects to rationalize marketing of fruits and vegetables and to improve the structure of the dairy industry. The third category combined the aims of the first two as applied to meat, wine production, olive growing, and the development of backward areas.

One of the most troublesome questions about the Guarantee and Guidance Fund is, Who gets the bulk of the monies? France, the major exporter of grain, has been the largest beneficiary of the export subsidy. Some of the smaller states such as the Netherlands have imported wheat and exported flour under subsidy. There are charges, as mentioned earlier, that commercial firms with the approval of their home governments (the governments must supply import licenses) are importing into the Market nearly twice as much wheat as the Market needs for domestic use, collecting high levies, and then exporting nearly 10 million tons of wheat on which export subsidies are paid from the Guarantee Fund. As far as the Guarantee and Guidance Fund expenditures for structural change are concerned, Italy and Greece seem to have been the greatest beneficiaries.

Chapter 11

THE ASSOCIATE STATES

MORE THAN FORTY sovereign nations and dependencies have sought some sort of affiliation with the Common Market. Each has been aware of the market potentials in the EC and the special position and economic advantage which affiliation with the Six brings. The Common Market has developed four types of economic relationships with outside areas.

FULL ASSOCIATE MEMBERSHIP

The first is full associate membership with the Common Market. This status grants all the preferences and privileges of the Six, and the Six are permitted free, unrestricted trade in the associate country. Of the more than twenty-five countries or dependencies which now have some sort of affiliation with the Common Market, only Greece has achieved the status of full associate membership so far as preferences are concerned.[1]

LIMITED ASSOCIATION

A second kind of relationship with the EC is a limited association arrangement. Such an arrangement allows preference for certain of the limited associate's goods, sometimes without corresponding concessions

---

1. Greece, however, has nearly twenty years to achieve full compliance with all of the monetary, legal, and nontariff regulations in the Market.

to the bill. Turkey is an example. The Market gives preference to Turkish tobacco, raisins, dried figs, and hazelnuts. Only a quota of 12,500 tons of tobacco receives this special treatment. The tobacco quota is divided among the Six on the basis of former imports of Turkish tobacco. The quota of course does not guarantee that 12,500 tons will be sold in the Common Market area; it is merely a permission to sell if the market exists. Tobacco from Turkey shipped into the Six above this quota bears the normal extended tariff, as defined by the Kennedy Round negotiations. Turkey is presently making a study of its industrial situation and other agricultural exports to determine what the effect of full associate status would mean. It is generally admitted that the rather inefficient and outmoded industry of Turkey could not withstand the competition of the more modern and dynamic industrial systems in the Six. Turkey is moving toward expanded production of fruits and vegetables in areas served by high dams presently under construction and is pressing for preferences on these products. Presently, fruit and vegetable imports into the Common Market are controlled by quality regulations within the Six rather than quotas. Turkey feels that her climatic and soil conditions will permit the production of superior items for this market. One Turkish experiment, however, illustrates a typical oversight of would-be associate nations—the potential of the home market. In the summer of 1968 Turkey produced and shipped to the EC and other European countries high-quality strawberries which were sold at quality prices. It was discovered that the tourist population and rising living standards in Turkey's major cities would absorb all the berries produced at a price even higher than was received, and with less cost and trouble in marketing. Both Greece and Turkey have special preference arrangements with the EC on citrus fruits. In the most recent agreement they pay a duty equal to 4 percent of the normal tariff, which is 20 percent. This applies only when the import price is above or equal to the reference price established by the Common Market. New agreements have also been negotiated with Israel and Spain for preference on fresh oranges, tangerines, mandarins, and similar citrus fruits (with the exception of grapefruit). The new arrangement gives these citrus-producing countries an 8 percent import preference over the United States and all other outside citrus-producing areas. In negotiations in early 1971 France sought and received similar special arrangements on citrus products for the former French colonies of Tunisia and Algeria. When the negotiations for enlarging the Common Market to at least ten full members began, Austria, Spain, Sweden, and Switzerland renewed their proposals for some sort of limited association or special preference for some of their products.

YAOUNDE CONVENTION AGREEMENT

A third kind of economic relationship with the Common Market is the kind of affiliation now enjoyed by eighteen African states and former colonies of France, Belgium, and the Netherlands. The African states were formerly affiliated with the Common Market as a result of the Yaounde Convention of 1963. This arrangement provided for preferences on certain African products: coffee, cocoa, palm oil, peanut oil, a host of minor fiber items, spices, and other tropical products. In addition these producers received substantial loans, grant funds, and technical assistance from the Guarantee Fund to modernize their marketing systems; diversify their agriculture; and improve the social, health, and educational structures of their countries. Funds totaling $800 million had been spent or committed to these areas during the five-year period ending May 31, 1969. The Yaounde Convention was extended another five years in 1969. There is constant pressure for expanding the preference list in each of these states.

The effects and operation of the Yaounde Convention over the years have been dramatic. Exports of African products under free entry have boomed, and each of the Common Market members has open entry into the markets of eighteen nations which not long before had been closed except to the colonial powers. Thus German agricultural machinery can compete with French agricultural machinery in fourteen former French colonies. Textiles from any of the Six may compete in the textile market (almost exclusively the province of Belgium before the Convention) of Belgium's three former colonies. The entrance into the Market of duty-free coffee from the African states has seriously affected exports of coffee from Latin America. In the case of Brazil this has amounted to losses of more than $150 million per year. South American cocoa is also seriously affected. For the present the Yaounde arrangements have not seriously affected U.S. trade with the Six, although pressure for increased quotas for peanut oil and palm oil may eventually cut into U.S. soybean exports.

The Common Market, preoccupied with mounting surpluses of agricultural products, wanted to do as little as possible to increase competition for their own products and were inclined to leave the whole issue of the desirability of trade preferences for African states to the United Nations Conference on Trade and Development (UNCTAD). In the end the Guarantee Fund was increased to $900 million, to be expended over the next five years on the economic development of the eighteen states. At the same time these states would sell to the Market under a small reduction in the tariffs and a slight increase in the quotas for agricultural products already on the preference list. The negotiations were complicated by U.S. pressure to end the "reverse preferences" on industrial products with which the African states compensated the Six.

During negotiations for renewal of the Yaounde Convention in the summer of 1968, and in informal discussions between the author and working-level officials of the Six, there was some concern that the Yaounde Convention agreement had operated to isolate the nations of Africa which were not signatories—nearly one-half of Africa—and to deny them a fair share of the European Common Market. There was clear evidence that the African countries outside the Convention felt they were being denied equal privileges with their neighbors.

In the two principal international conferences of UNCTAD held in the past years, the developing countries have argued strongly for non-reciprocal trade preferences rather than foreign aid or grants under the present restrictive system. The lack of enthusiasm in Africa for the current agreement with the eighteen indicates a desire to move away from special trade preferences for specific nations and toward a common African trade advantage on a much larger list of goods.

SPECIAL AFFILIATIONS

Three other states—Iran, Israel, and Portugal—have sought some undetermined sort of relationship to increase entry of their goods into the Common Market area in return for more liberal regulations in their home markets. Iran and Israel have bilateral treaties with the Community containing most-favored-nation provisions. The most recent agreements on citrus with Spain and Israel are special arrangements outside the bilateral treaties.

NIGERIAN PATTERN

Nigeria, one of the African states of the British Commonwealth, early sought an affiliation independent of British application for membership in the Common Market. Presumably, British entry would have placed Nigeria in a special category similar to the former French and Belgian colonies. But when British entry was blocked, Nigeria made a separate application and was accepted as an affiliate. A similar arrangement was made with Morocco and Tunisia. The Nigerian arrangement was completed in 1965 but remained inoperative and finally expired in 1970 for lack of ratification, but the association agreement did set a pattern for other African states not parties to the Yaounde Convention. It was a new kind of relationship with the Common Market and deserves some further explanation. Nigeria was to be more independent economically of other Market affiliates, and there were fewer institutional features than in the arrangement with the eighteen former French, Dutch, and Belgian colonies. The agreement provided that Nigerian exports would have free entry into the Common Market, but some of the most important—cocoa, peanut oil, palm oil, and plywood—would enter duty free only in amounts equal to Nigerian exports to the Six during the three-year period 1962–64. These quotas were to be increased by 3 percent each year. Imports of these items in excess of the quotas were subject to a 5–15 percent duty. Nigeria for her part allowed preferential treatment to twenty-six items of commerce from the Six, reserving the right on occasion to apply quotas and levy taxes to protect infant industries or raise money. Unlike the nations which signed the Yaounde Convention, Nigeria had a very limited representation in Brussels and was accorded no investment or technical assistance by the Guarantee Fund. However, she was not limited in her association with any of the other African states. The emphasis in the Nigerian agreement was on trade rather than political ties or involvement in the institutions of the Community.

ARSHUA CONVENTION

In July 1968 three East African countries—Kenya, Uganda, and Tanzania—signed an association convention with the European Community at Arshua. The agreement provided for a wide assortment of trade preferences on a variety of products. It ran for one year and was renewed at the end of 1969. In general the agreement allowed these East African countries' exports to enter the Community duty free, except that (as in the case of the Nigerian agreement) quotas were applied to coffee, peanut oil, cloves, canned pineapple, and a few other items. In turn the East African countries agreed to grant tariff concessions on some sixty Common Market products. The agreement is implemented through a joint Association Council which meets periodically.

OTHER SPECIAL ARRANGEMENTS

These special arrangements of association by African states under the Yaounde Convention, the Nigerian scheme, and the Arshua Convention have renewed pressure by all the other African states and some developing countries for special treatment on tariff duties. Taking note of this rising pressure, the Council of Ministers of the European Community late in March 1971, in cooperation with UNCTAD, worked out a generalized preference system on semiprocessed and manufactured items from 91 developing countries. Agricultural products were not included in the arrangement, but consideration is to be given to semiprocessed agricultural items in the future. This industrial tariff preference affects trade between the 91 countries and the EC amounting to almost $1 billion per year. The EC expects to lose about $100 million in duties under this arrangement. Seven other countries (not necessarily underdeveloped)—Israel, Portugal, Spain, Turkey, Malta, Taiwan, and Cuba—are seeking the same arrangement. Discussions along this line are going on between these countries and the EC within the framework of the Organization for Economic Cooperation and Development (OECD). These arrangements have done much to unfreeze patterns of the European-African trade relationships which have until recently followed pretty well the colonial pattern. The extension by the EC of these trade preferences on industrial goods to Latin American and Asian

countries increases the pressure on the United States and other indus
trial countries for similar concessions. With the final formal admittance
of Great Britain, Norway, Denmark, and Ireland in 1973, pressure for
some sort of worldwide preference system will be increased. The United
States at the UNCTAD meetings in recent years has always opposed
the generalized preference system in favor of some sort of worldwide
fixed tariff under the General Agreement on Tariffs and Trade
(GATT). However, trends in the EC toward even greater use of preference arrangements with countries of special interest to the Community
places the United States, Canada, Japan, and other industrialized countries outside the EC in marked disadvantage on all types of trade.

Since generalized preferences by the European Community do not
include agricultural products, negotiations for preferences (as in the
case of cocoa, spices, and palm oil from Nigeria) are to be conducted
under the Common Agricultural Policy. Only one of the Eastern European states—Yugoslavia (already with a limited association with the
EC)—is included in the generalized preference arrangement. However,
Eastern Europe is pressing for a common commercial trade policy with
the Common Market, and at least four of these countries—Poland, Hungary, Czechoslovakia, and Romania—are gearing their economies to wider
trade with the Community. Presently trade between Eastern European
nations and individual states of the Six is on the basis of bilateral barter.
The exchange of goods between the areas is virtually balanced out each
year. Italy, for example, wanting to trade with Hungary, sells Fiat cars
or other industrial goods up to an agreed amount each year and in
return takes from Hungary an exactly equal value of fruits, meat products, timber, and other materials. It was in 1970 that Yugoslavia became
the first and only Eastern European country to be admitted to the list
of states with special preference arrangements. The arrangement gives
Yugoslavia an annual quota in the Community's live beef and veal
market. With the enlargement of the Community, pressures will mount
for more special arrangements and preferences. Austria, for example,
now enjoys some preference for its timber products because of special
arrangements with Germany early in the transition period. Sweden
wants entry for some of her live cattle and other agricultural products
but is reluctant to seek a formal relationship, fearing the growing interest in political and fiscal unity might jeopardize her neutral position.
Norway demanded and got, as a condition of her association agreement,
special arrangements for fish products. Switzerland, with 45 percent of
her international trade with the Common Market, will undoubtedly
seek some special status.

Chapter 12

AGRICULTURAL CHANGES IN EASTERN EUROPE

THE AGRICULTURAL STRUCTURE presently emerging in Eastern Europe may well be as revolutionary and far reaching as the political changes instituted by the Communists in the years immediately following World War II. The imposition of the Soviet economic and political system on agriculture all but destroyed the age-old pattern of large estates, elite ownership, commercial farming of crops easily salable in world markets on the one hand, and the hordes of peasant small holders whose objective was sheer survival on the other. In recent years this new revolution in economics has evolved toward the adoption of a modified market economy in Eastern Europe. Except in the minds of a few doctrinaire individuals who look at the word *Communist* first and disregard everything else, the illusion of a Communist-dominated Eastern Europe tied irrevocably to Russia has also vanished. Gone also is the illusion, except among a few diplomats who parrot the official line, that there is a solid economic, political, and military base in the West.

Both the NATO-Atlantic Community concept and the Council for Mutual Cooperation (Comecon) of Eastern Europe are in some disarray.[1]

---

1. Comecon, established some twenty years ago, was theoretically the Communist bloc's answer to the Organization for Economic Cooperation and Development (OECD) and the Common Market. While visualized as an integrated system similar to the Common Market, Comecon has never operated in that manner. The six major Eastern European states of Bulgaria, Romania, Hungary, Czechoslovakia, Poland, and Yugoslavia plus Eastern Germany have insisted on broad cooperation in certain areas with eventual multilateral adjustment rather than coordination and integration. While still heavily oriented toward Russia in trade and international politics, each of the Eastern European states insists on broader contacts all along the line with Western countries. Latest developments in the area of trade for the Communist bloc came late in 1970

91

Out of these changes may emerge a Europe tied into some sort of a structure—with certain limited compromises and political overtones—which complements the historical, economic, cultural, and priority interests of the individual states rather than political ideology.

The agricultural sector in both Eastern and Western Europe has always been one of the most difficult areas to bring under political or ideological control. One need only recall the Fascist system imposed on Italy, the Nazi system with its intricately planned Reichnahrstrand (food and agriculture) production and distribution system, or the collectivized system inaugurated in Russia fifty years ago and later imposed on the states of Eastern Europe. By the same token, the agricultural sector usually has been the first to throw off the restrictive bonds of these rigidly controlled and centrally planned systems. No doubt this independence is the result of the very human and timeless tradition of men of the soil who want some say about how they go about planting their crops, based on their judgment of what is best for themselves and their families. The pattern of transformation in agriculture in almost any country which was forced to accept the Soviet system is fairly predictable as to both form and results. This pattern of transformation is evident not only in countries under Communist control but in countries such as Ghana where Soviet technicians and commissars were called in to help the country adjust its economy.

Soviet System

The first step in the Soviet pattern is usually the takeover of the larger estates either by seizure, purchase, or common contract. In some countries this involves confiscation of land areas of several thousand acres; in other countries, where a series of land reforms has reduced individual holdings to a minimum, it involves confiscation of plats as small as fifty acres. The land in these estates is usually allocated three ways: (1) The tenants or workers on the estate are allowed to buy or contract for a minimum acreage, usually an area sufficient to support a family in that particular country. In Eastern Europe it is usually 5–20 acres. (2) A portion of the estate is put into the national land pool to be distributed to those who have no land at all or to be added to the small holdings of individual farmers. (3) The owner of the estate, if he is a native, is allowed the central house and 50–200 acres, depending on the country and his political leanings. In most instances this is where the matter stops the first year. The new farm owners must scrounge

---

when Russia and her economic partners opened a $1.1 billion International Investment Bank with nearly half the paid-in capital in gold and Western hard currencies. Financial experts in the West see this move as one aimed at raising funds by conventional sources of trade and international exchange rather than through sale of gold in the West. It emphasizes the move in the Eastern group to seek funds and resources for economic expansion and technical developments in the capitalist countries of the West.

for their seed, equipment, credit, and other inputs. The former owner sometimes leases some of the land from the new owners and farms it. The disruptions of this procedure inevitably result in poor production. The failure of the new owners to produce their quota of products means that they are unable to pay in kind the loans they received to take over the land. The next step is voluntary collectivization. The state offers credit, supervision, a guaranteed wage, and equipment from a machine station if the new owners will pool their resources. They retain title to their holdings, which they have not yet paid for. Under the system each is allowed a small private plot that he can work by hand, and each can keep a limited number of livestock, chickens, honeybees, guinea fowl, and fruit trees. The contract in this voluntary collective usually runs for a period of five years, at the end of which the owner may withdraw from the arrangement. However, at this point the state really takes over. Production plans are drawn up at the central bureaucracy; managers or supervisors—originally all party men—are sent out to plan not only the specifics of what shall be planted but where, what kind, how much must be produced, and how many persons must work on a given project. Squads and battalions of workers are organized; each squad is given a norm; there is much marching to and from the field; and the show is on.

The estate takeover is usually the easiest step in the Soviet collectivization scheme. After the estates, the Soviets must deal with the peasants on fragmented farms of one- or two-hectare strips outside the rural villages. (Occasionally peasant farms in Eastern Europe consisted of as much as fifteen or twenty hectares, rarely more than that.) Again, the collectivization process is hailed as voluntary. Each small holder places his land in a pool but retains title and ownership. He puts his horses, oxen, wagons, tools, and other equipment into the central pool and is paid in cash or given credit for this contribution. The local agencies of the village such as cooperatives for credit, marketing, procurement of inputs, and machinery hire—which had previously supported his farm operations—are immediately abolished or taken over by the state. These local cooperatives flourished throughout Eastern Europe between World War I and World War II and were the base for much of the political agitation and revolts among the peasants during that stormy period. The functions of the local cooperatives are taken over by a series of state agencies which take orders directly from the bureaucracies and planning ministries in the country involved. Credit is supplied by one agency; a machine station is created and managed by another agency; marketing is done by another agency; prices are set by another; production planning is done by another; and wages, salaries, and production norms are set up by another. Since large-scale management ability is limited in nearly all countries, particularly in Eastern Europe, the real management comes from the central office, largely in theoretical form. In the early days the people (mostly party hacks) sent out to manage the collectives were little more than paper pushers and order takers. Calls came from the top to plant so many acres of corn. Whether or not corn grew well in the area, whether oats would grow better, corn was planted. Machines from the machine station might be ordered out to cut the crop, but someone in the bureaucracy responsible for the petroleum to run the machines could be on vacation or simply forget, with the result that often the machines stood idle in the field while the wheat or corn or oats rotted. Planting time might come, and with it the discovery that someone had failed to order the needed seed in time to be planted. Inevitably such a system would be disappointing in most cases and an utter failure in others. Since the government had made all the plans and the workers and former owners had followed the orders, and a failure occurred anyway, the peasant—now a worker for wages—took no responsibility for the failure. He gave his attention to his small plot which at least enabled him to eat and survive another year.

These were the developments which generally occurred in each of the countries during the first five-year period of the collectivization effort. The theory, however, was that the collective system would be so successful that the former owners would either sell or donate their small plots to the state and the aggregate would become a state farm owned by all the people with the peasant, a worker on the land, getting equal pay and equal status with his brother worker in the city. In a majority of cases the peasants who contracted for parcels of land on the great estates and then joined the collectives did donate their land. They had nothing invested and were unable to pay for it anyway. In most instances these former large estates became state farms. The method of transforming these estates into state farms varied from country to country. In the case of Hungary and Poland (and to some extent Romania and Czechoslovakia) the technique was ruthless, often involving imprisonment of the former owners and imposition of quotas on the new owners which they could not possibly meet. Unfilled quotas opened the way for the state to take over. In other countries such as Bulgaria the process was more humane, entirely legal, and relatively painless for the estate owners (who were relatively few in number). Yugoslavia took over foreign estates, municipal holdings, church lands, and other parcels of good land in the Danube basin without much disruption but was stopped cold in collectivization when it came to the small peasant holdings around the thousands of rural villages in the hill country.

By and large the centrally imposed, centrally planned, rigidly controlled system failed to produce results for the state. It was even more disappointing to the little people who joined the collective believing that large-scale, more extensive agriculture would result in improved income and better living conditions for themselves and the families in their village. The result was that in some of the countries, Yugoslavia and Poland in particular, the peasants took advantage of the escape clause in their contracts and withdrew from the collectives in droves. By early 1970 fewer than 10 percent of the collectives were in existence in Yugoslavia and Poland.

Faced with mounting deficits, low production, and actual disintegration of collectives, the central powers in each country began to yield to small but important alterations in the system. Among the first changes was elimination of the machine stations, which had become a sort of a symbol of the new agriculture. Except for some very heavy equipment, collectives were allowed to purchase, maintain, and manage their own machinery. The former machine stations were usually converted to repair stations. In Poland, where thirty-two machine stations were set up and manned in as many districts, the stations now repair machinery for the cooperatives and state farms and operate mobile units which go out to private farms, circles, and cooperatives to make minor repairs on the spot and move equipment in need of overhaul or major repair to the central station. Special training courses are held regularly in machine maintenance, operation, and repair; in off-seasons the sometimes elaborate and extensive equipment in these stations is used to mill small parts for the state-operated tractor factory. There has also been gradual abandonment of fixed uniform wages, and more attention has been given to increased payment for special skills and productivity.

General Farm Cooperative System

Not until the late 1960s did a fundamental change in the direction and method of managing agriculture begin to take shape. Some years earlier Yugoslavia had placed its hope for large-scale commercial production on the expansion of the state farms. The government began buying out retired farmers, purchasing church and municipal lands, and reclaiming vast stretches of swamp in the Danube basin. At about the same time the idea of a General Farm Cooperative took hold with the former participants in collective farms, and this became the second major basis for development of Yugoslav agriculture. The General Farm Cooperative is just about what the name implies. The small holders voluntarily place their land in a pool from which they draw rent on the basis of size of holding and productivity of land. Major machinery is pooled as in the Soviet collective, and small plots for individual use are retained in the system. But in other respects the system is radically different from past experiments. Control is at the local level. A general assembly of all members selects a board of directors or a council. This is the basic governing body which lays down policy, hires management, and selects the technicians required to assist in the farming program. Minimum wages are paid in cash weekly on the basis of number of days worked, work accomplished, and skills required. The small plots no longer have to depend strictly on hand labor to look after them. The central cooperative office supplies seeds and fertilizers, machinery is available for hire, and transportation of the products to the city markets is provided. Overall cropping plans are made on the basis of a broad national goal set up by the state but are largely implemented on the basis of what will find the best market and provide the largest income. Gross land taxes and gross income taxes are paid to the state. Interest is paid on borrowed money, which has been borrowed where it could be secured most conveniently. Bonuses at the end of the year are paid to the workers on a net profit basis; the recipient of the bonus may take it in cash, donate it to the central cultural fund, leave it in the cooperative as working capital to draw interest, or increase his own contribution to a pension fund which the state matches. In most cases the cooperative determines the required contribution to the pension fund, and the decision depends largely on the profitability of the enterprise.

While this system started in Yugoslavia, it is now used in all of the countries to varying degrees. Collectives which have survived are now gradually converting to the General Farm Cooperative system of self-sustaining, self-governing, and managed enterprise. Bulgaria, which had a long history of land reform and agitation and a vast network of general-service, privately owned cooperatives, never did completely accept the Soviet pattern of land reform. Adaptations were made to suit Soviet doctrine; at the same time many features of the former system were retained and strengthened with state aid. The result has been that Bulgaria is almost the only country in the Eastern bloc to experience a steady increase in agricultural production and has developed one of the most diversified agricultural systems in Eastern Europe. Romania has probably been the most successful with the Soviet system, due largely to her enormous agricultural resources. Yet here too, change has come. With new economic, planning, and management methods now being accepted in all phases of the society, Romania is completely decentralizing its planning, management, marketing, and pricing systems and at the same time is setting up central management, supply, and marketing cooperatives which stand between the government and new cooperatives operating on the General Farm Cooperative principle. Farmer-controlled and -managed enterprises may make contracts with the Romanian government, an exporting agency, or a foreign firm for sale of products or purchases of imports. The Communist party still controls the government in all these countries. No doubt party members are involved in the councils and other government bodies connected with agriculture; but many of the managers and local councils will attest that, outside of broad policy lines, the party no longer interferes with day-to-day operations. More and more, the young college graduates and technically trained people are determining what is or is not done. The central planning offices for agriculture in Hungary and two or three other countries have been abolished. Elaborate training institutes dealing with management, production, care and maintenance of machinery, and use of fertilizers and herbicides are in evidence everywhere. Under the original collectivist doctrine, the small plots would eventually disappear along with the individual ownership of the land. Nothing like that is talked about or even hinted now. The small plots and individual owner-ship of land seem to be a standard and fixed part of the system. In Bul-garia at least, and to a limited degree in all the others, provision is made for a family to leave the land in the pool and receive substantial interest and production returns even though the family has quit farming and moved to the city. In Czechoslovakia small plot owners are encouraged to make use of their small plots to the maximum in the production of livestock, poultry, honeybees, fruits, vegetables, and all other crops not adaptable to mass or extensive production methods. Even under the old restrictive system these small plots were important sources of income for those in the collective or cooperative. As late as 1960, before the liberalization of the small plot regulations, a study by the Hungarian Central Bureau of Statistics involving 26,000 cooperative or collective members showed that 50.6 percent of the total individual family income came from the private plots. About 7 percent of the income came from rent on their land in the pool, and the remainder came from wages earned by members of the family on the cooperative farm. It was also revealed that 35 percent of all families had one or more members work-ing outside the farm for wages.

Until the early 1970s, before the changes in price systems and other reforms began to take place, agricultural development generally was given much lip service and considerable development credit in the form of rather ambitious machinery and development schemes. The rural population was exploited by means of ridiculous prices and failure to provide the necessary roads, schools, irrigation, health services, transpor-tation, and communications which a modern agriculture requires. High wages and better living conditions in the cities drew droves of younger people to the cities and towns. It was not possible to mechanize and modernize agriculture fast enough to offset this drain of manpower. Pro-duction obviously suffered, although official statistics always managed to show gains of some kind. The fraud of Eastern European statistics on agricultural production lay chiefly in the fact that the statistics against which production was compared were those from the immediate post-war years when Eastern Europe was emerging not only from war but from the vast chaos of the Communist takeover. It was not until the mid-1960s that a single crop in a single country approached the pro-duction of 1938, the last prewar year. The rising living standards in Eastern European cities have created demands for new types of food. The agricultural sector, therefore, has pushed the production of meat, dairy and poultry products, fruits, and vegetables upward and deempha-sized the traditional cash crops of sugar, wheat, barley, oilseeds, corn, oats, and potatoes. Only two countries in the group now seem to be emphasizing the traditional cereals; Romania and Yugoslavia are mak-ing an effort to sell corn to Western European countries. The Eastern European bloc presently is deficient in several of the cereals it has tra-ditionally exported.

Modernization

The manpower shortage in the countryside as young people have left for higher wages and better living standards in the towns and cities has caused party councils to reexamine the whole agricultural situation. The advice of younger intellectuals and hard-fisted managers who were trying to make the farms produce has prevailed over the theorists and central bureaucrats. In all countries the result has been heavy investment and new interest in making rural life and agriculture in particular more attractive. Attractive home-building schemes have been publicized which enable small landowners, whether or not they were in a cooperative, to borrow money at 2 percent for forty years to build a new home. Literally hundreds of thousands of such units have gone up in the rural villages; nearly all of them have inside running water, and 85 percent have electrical service. Vast sums are being allocated to what one would call "farm-to-market roads." Lack of transportation and storage has been a severe bottleneck to the development of extensive agriculture in Eastern Europe. Under the old traditional pattern, each small farmer harvested his small acreage by hand and brought it to the market in a cart or wagon over a period of weeks or months. Under the modern system, of course, harvested crops must be brought to storage or market within a few days.

Nearly 20 percent of the state budget in some of the countries now goes to education, an increasing part of it to rural villages. Romania, one of the most backward of the Eastern European states but rich in resources, has shown industrial growth of about 12 percent per year for many years. Until recently agriculture has lagged, but under a new system of pricing which offers more production incentives and a decentralized management, the land resources of that country are beginning to pay off. The party is no longer permitted to interfere with the day-to-day management of either farm or factory. In Romania and Bulgaria farmers have created cooperative associations or bureaus designed to undertake land improvement; provide extension services, storage, and processing facilities; and to buy and sell on behalf of the members.

HUNGARIAN MANIFESTO

Just what is implied in this new economic, management, and planning system? Excerpts from a manifesto issued in Hungary in 1966, which set the deadline for full implementation of the new system in 1968, suggest some of the implications:

> Central programming of production is to be abolished in agriculture, mining, and industry.
> Rationing as a system of distribution is to be abolished.

Central allocation of investment is to be abolished.
Administered prices and wages are to be abolished.
The profit motive is to be restored.

In addition, the plan calls for eventual lifting of all currency exchange restrictions. About the only difference between this system and that which exists in the West is that in the West profits, property, and prices go directly to the individuals; under the Eastern system the rewards go to groups, enterprises, and state cooperatives and then to the individual through wages or other embellishments.

EFFECTS

The question remains: What will be the long-term effects of this new system on the economic and/or political system in these countries? First, one may well assume that for some time to come there will be no blossoming of a liberal democracy. But it is already evident that the party has lost control of the economics of the countries, and only to the extent that government policy can influence growth and development will the party hand be felt in the day-to-day economic affairs of these countries. Second, movement toward the profit system means a market-oriented economy. These countries will tend more and more to produce the products that can be sold at a profit. The younger trading managers envision the day when they will sell where the price is best and buy where it is most profitable—and all this without regard to ideological and political considerations. The decentralization of production planning in the agricultural sector has already resulted in vastly more efficient use of resources and labor. One cooperative farm manager has remarked that by careful scheduling of the work and because of the freedom to buy and manage his own equipment, his farm was using only twelve tractors where they had once used twenty-five. By permitting centralized transportation to collect and haul to market the produce from the small plots, many man-hours are saved and a better quality and grade of product reaches the market. Increased and more efficient use of inputs and better management, plus some assist from weather, have caused an increase in output for market since about 1964. Production increases prior to that time ranged from 1 to 3 percent per year. In the past five years they have averaged more than 5 percent, and in some countries as high as 9 percent.

Eastern Europe's 1968 production, including East Germany, was 30 percent above the 1957–59 base.[2] The production in 1970 reached new peaks in all countries except Czechoslovakia and East Germany. Ap-

---

2. *Eastern Europe's Agricultural Development and Trade,* Economic Research Service, USDA, July 1970.

plication of improved technology has also increased. Use of fertilizer has increased at an annual rate of 10 percent; tractors by about 12 percent. Wheat and sugar have shown the greatest increases in production, but increases have occurred across the spectrum. The increased demand of the people for nongrain products is reflected in the total agricultural products imports of $3.5 billion in 1969, more than three-fourths of which were in the nongrain items. At the same time exports of agricultural products have been increasing faster than imports; 10 percent per year for exports against 6.4 percent for imports. The U.S. share of this trade is small (less than 8 percent of the total) with Poland and Yugoslavia the main customers.

It now appears that most of the dislocation and confusion of the early 1950s and the upheavals of the early 1960s are history. The present agricultural system of Eastern Europe is likely to produce a more stable growth pattern, although probably not at the peak rates some of the countries have enjoyed in recent years.

Chapter 13

UNITED STATES AND EASTERN EUROPEAN

TRADE POLICIES

SOVIET INTERVENTION in the political and economic reform movement of Czechoslovakia slowed down but did not stop the six Eastern European countries—Bulgaria, Romania, Hungary, Yugoslavia, Poland, and Czechoslovakia—in their efforts for closer economic ties with Western European nations. As early as 1947 Yugoslavia refused to perform as a puppet of Stalin and broke away from the rigid system by accepting economic and military assistance from the United States and other Western nations. Since then Yugoslavia has been the leader in economic and political reform in the Communist bloc. Each of the other Eastern European countries has had its periods of restiveness and rebellion against the tight controls and economic and military ties with Russia. However, it was not until the introduction of the new economic planning and management policies in 1966 that the ties holding these areas to Russia began to weaken significantly. The changes in the economic system discussed in Chapter 12 set in motion a sense of independence and freedom which infiltrated every level of the social system, especially among the youth and the younger managers of various enterprises. The private sector, always a factor but often ignored, found new relationships with the state monoliths; private and state enterprises began to merge as a result of the day-to-day contacts. Price reforms made small private enterprises more attractive.

Private establishments in commerce, industry, agriculture, mining, and transportation in each country are limited to a maximum of five

101

employed persons. In actual fact these private establishments comprise
a huge component of the total economic strength of each country. Ideo-
logically, militarily, and economically Eastern Europe is tied to Russia,
but each country's heritage is closer to that of Western European countries. In the years since World War II exchange of goods between Eastern Europe (including Russia) with Western nations has reached more
than $10 billion annually and is growing. In most recent statistics of
the European Free Trade Association (EFTA) the highest increase in
trade for any area was with Eastern Europe, a 14 percent gain. The
highest gain for any other area was 4 percent.

ECONOMIC CHANGES

Probably the Czech-Russian crisis of 1968 grew out of the Czech
attempt to go beyond the new economics as much as anything else. In
a great surge to reequip their run-down industries and to increase sales
with the West, Czechoslovakia, Yugoslavia, possibly Hungary, and even
Romania were on the verge of establishing an International Bank. In
the summer of 1964 these four countries were quietly making plans to
place their currency on an international exchange basis. As one high
Czech bureaucrat observed to this writer in 1967, "If we are to establish
in this country a truly market economy, then we must buy where we can
buy best and sell where we can sell for the most profit. This also means
our currency must have an exchange value in the international market
and must be subject to the disciplines of that market." Czechoslovakia
not only was moving fast toward a new economic position but was ac-
companying the move with new political, press, art, and cultural free-
doms and making considerable noise about it. Apparently the Russians
could not tolerate the combination for reasons of politics, ideology, and
military security.

Twenty-five years of effort on the part of the Russians has not
made the Eastern European countries total satellites. Below the top
echelon of policy makers, changes are occurring which in time will profoundly alter this part of the world. Bulgaria—for many reasons one of
the most docile of the group—long ago rejected the Stalinist system in
agriculture, diversified, and adopted a voluntary cooperative system
which has transformed that agricultural economy into a relatively prosperous one with a wide variety of agricultural products moving into
world markets. Hungary, without fanfare, probably has gone as far in
adopting the new economics and working toward a truly market economy as any of the states in this bloc. This has been going on under a
relatively benevolent Communist dictatorship which, while giving lip
service to the Russian line, is quietly encouraging more and more trade
and cultural ties with the Western nations. One of the biggest hits in
Budapest in the summer of 1967 was an Italian opera company which

gave concerts in the moonlit stadium on an island in the Danube. The hotels swarmed with Western European and Japanese trade delegations selling their wares.

U.S. POLICY

During this period the United States has not enjoyed cultural contacts or, until most recently, exchange of goods on any significant scale. International trade between the United States and the entire Communist bloc has rarely exceeded $200 million in any one year. Perhaps the policy adopted by the United States after the close of World War II to halt the spread of communism is the major reason for this situation. The strained cooperation between Russia and the Western Allies which held together during the fighting in World War II began to evaporate when hostilities ceased. From that period until the "building of bridges" statement by President Johnson in 1966, our policy has generally been characterized as restrictive and negative. Such a course has not been conducive to communication or trade with countries associated with the Communist bloc.

Late in 1947 when there was a food crisis in a large part of Western Europe, a staff member of the U.S. military government in Germany who was responsible for trade and commerce vetoed a barter agreement between West Germany and Yugoslavia whereby German tractor frames and parts would be exchanged for an estimated 300,000 tons of corn from the Danube basin. The argument was that "the tractor frames could easily be converted into light tanks . . . we want to make it as difficult as possible for these people to get going again because they are not on our side." This was before the cold war reached its zenith, but the incident is illustrative of U.S. policy toward Eastern Europe for the past twenty-five years—to hold commercial relationships between the two blocs to a minimum and to deny in particular anything which might help the area to industrialize or develop its military strength. The original lists of strategic materials drawn up by the U.S. Commerce Department and the Defense Department indicated that practically everything from sewing machines to telephone equipment had military potential and therefore should not be sold by any member of the North Atlantic Treaty Organization (NATO) to the Soviet bloc. As one trader put it, this left only toothpaste and candy bars for international commerce. Whether this policy was self-defeating or materially stifled the reconstruction of the Soviet bloc will be a debate of long standing. The facts are that through deft use of third countries and dummy corporations in NATO countries and neutral countries, the Communist group did get the ball bearings and the technical equipment which Russia needed for rearmament. Russia did create its own atomic bomb, the first Sputnik, and more recently a fleet which encompasses the seven seas. How effective U.S. policy has been is best left for historians of the future to decide. However, it has long been clear that most allies of the United States were less than enthusiastic about the policy of nontrade with the Eastern bloc. From the beginning, each tiny crack in the trade barrier developed into a river as the years went on—and through the efforts of U.S. allies. With the "building of bridges" policy of President Johnson in early 1966 the rush of U.S. allies to trade in the East reached the proportions of a campaign.

CMEA

If the Western boycott of trade has failed in recent years, CMEA[1] (the Soviet answer to the Common Market and U.S. nontrade policy) is in similar confusion and disruption. CMEA is the alphabetical designation for Council for Mutual Economic Assistance and was conceived as a customs union based primarily on bilateral trade agreements between members of the bloc. CMEA also incorporated a major Soviet plan of integrating the economies of the Eastern European states with that of the Soviet Union.[2] Each nation, according to the idea, would contribute what it could produce best within the whole. Thus some Eastern European countries—Romania, Bulgaria, and Hungary—would become the main agricultural producers. Czechoslovakia and Poland with minerals, fuel, and major industrial capacity would produce industrial goods. Above this whole structure, the International Bank of Economic Cooperation (according to the Soviet plan) would tie together regional economies and trade and provide for multilateral settlement of trade balances. Under the existing bilateral systems between an industrial country and an agricultural country, trade has to balance out evenly if there is to be no deficit on one side or the other. Yet there is always a period of deficit in such a relationship, since the industrial goods usually come in throughout the year and the agricultural goods which repay the balance come once a year. The multilateral arrangement under the International Bank of Economic Cooperation broadens the general area of trade although it does not necessarily give priority to trade expansion. Rather, the system was designed to produce self-sufficiency as far as possible in both industrial and agricultural goods, and this purpose affected Bank attitudes toward trade with non-Communist countries. The Bank as visualized at the time of its establishment in 1964 has virtually failed as one Eastern European country after another has insisted on greater trade with non-Communist countries.

---

1. CMEA and Comecon designate the same institution and are used interchangeably.
2. At the most recent meeting of the members of CMEA the issue of complete economic integration was again shelved. However, the communique issued after the meeting indicated that some agreement had been reached on more coordination of economic development and trade policies.

Romania, for example, refuses to sell its corn, wheat, and oilseeds to Czechoslovakia and Poland which need them. Romania instead insists on trading with Israel, Japan, Austria, West Germany, England, and Switzerland where industrial and technical products needed by Romania are available. Increased demand of certain industrial goods is another important reason commerce between East and West has developed so rapidly. This increased trade with Western nations, however, has somewhat split the Eastern bloc. At the summit meeting of the East European countries late in 1969 the split between the so-called progressive socialist and the conservative groups was further widened when Russia, Bulgaria, and East Germany found Yugoslavia and Romania both mavericks on the international trade. Hungary, Czechoslovakia, and Poland joined the debate for abolition of the "limited sovereignty theory" so far as economic matters were concerned. There was not only a strong protest against the rigid bilateral trade system of CMEA on internal matters but an even stronger effort to broaden the scope of international trade with the outside world. This involved ruble convertibility and attendant eventual convertibility of the currencies of each of the bloc countries. It was pointed out that the Soviet bloc now produces 31 percent of the world's goods but is involved in only 11 percent of the international trade. In spite of pressure by Russia to restrain trade with the Western nations and to force the bloc nations to perform according to ideological pattern, each country is increasing its contact with the West by every known means of trade manipulation.

SWITCH ACCOUNT SYSTEM

A device widely used to skirt the bilateral and barter approach is the so-called switch account, widely used by Western European nations just after World War II when few Western European currencies were convertible and trade was still on a limited barter or bilateral basis. The switch account is a logical forerunner of convertibility. In the case of Eastern Europe it works as follows: An Eastern European country may enter a trade agreement with an African nation (or even a developed country) for a general level of trade, involving perhaps industrial goods for raw materials. The African country may find itself with more credit in Eastern European currency than it cares to spend on industrial goods from the Eastern European country. A Western firm wants to sell the African country some goods which the African country needs but cannot purchase for lack of hard currency. The Western dealer raises the prices on his goods and takes the Eastern European currency or credit in payment, hoping to "switch," that is, to find a business firm in a hard currency country that needs Eastern European currency for purchases in the bloc. When such a firm is located, it buys the Eastern European money or credit with hard currency but at a discount. The original exporter to the African country than he had hard currency, and the second exporter has secured credits or currency for purchases in the Eastern European country. Though complicated, each party received what he wanted in the European country. Business of this kind is increasing in volume, and now there has been created a "clearing dollar"; it is not convertible but is merely an item on the books and a sort of yardstick to facilitate switching which may involve half a dozen countries and currencies before all the deals are completed.

How this system works on a large scale within a given country is recounted in the July 1970 issue of *Foreign Affairs* by Marshall I. Goldman. The International Hotel Corporation wanted to build and operate a hotel in Budapest. After some difficulty, Tower International, an American commission firm, negotiated an agreement with the Hungarian National Planning Commission for the construction of a hotel with the stipulation that it would be financed with hard currency. With this commitment, Tower International went to the Foreign Trade Bank of Hungary which agreed that if the hotel were built, a minimum yearly amount of the payments would be turned over to the builders. Armed with this guarantee, the American firm went to the Moscow Bank Limited in London and secured $6 million credit in hard currency to build the hotel. Thus, in spite of official restrictions, red tape, and U.S. policy, firms are trading and dealing—presumably with profit—in Eastern Europe.

REORIENTATION OF TRADE

The impact of this activity in Western Europe may be seen from the trade statistics of the Economic Commission for Europe for the period 1965 to first half of 1967. Sales of Western European countries to Eastern Europe totaled $4,294,800,000, of which $1,789,200,000 was credited to the Soviet Union. Bulgaria bought over $216 million worth of goods from the West and sold the West more than $342 million worth; Czechoslovakia bought over $511 million and sold over $522 million; Hungary bought over $808 million and sold over $817 million. Poland bought $702 million and sold $591 million; Romania bought $336 million and sold $373 million. Only Poland and Hungary had deficit trade balances with the West during the period. For the first half of 1967 only the Soviet Union showed a trade deficit with the West. The Soviet bloc area was both a large importer of agricultural products from the West and a major exporter of some agricultural products. In terms of dollars Eastern Europe in 1966 imported fats and oils, food, beverages, and oilseeds valued at more than $926 million; of this, $157 million worth went to the Soviet Union. Livestock and dairy products accounted for $481 million plus, with only $20 million worth going to the Soviet Union. Cereals, flour, and bran amounting to $95 million were imported, and $159 million worth were exported in 1966. Fruit, vegetables, and tobacco imported from Western Europe in 1966 accounted for over $187 million; exports to Western Europe of these items amounted to more than $185 million. Eastern Europe imported sugar and other miscellaneous agricultural items totaling more than $209 million and exported only about $90 million.

While these statistics may seem small in terms of total world trade of the Eastern European bloc, they reflect an impressive development and reorientation of trade toward Western Europe. A striking feature of the trade is that the trade organizations and planners instead of pushing for the traditional exports of cereals, oilseeds, and sugar have conducted the bulk of the agricultural trade in semiprocessed livestock products. A rising volume of fruits, vegetables, and exotics—both fresh and processed—is under way. A survey conducted by this writer in 1967 indicated quite clearly that Eastern Europe's plans for export of agricultural products call for selectivity and high-value items aimed at a specific market rather than the broad basic exports of postwar years when sugar, wheat, barley, rape, and sunflower seed represented the bulk of the exports. Hungary has established a national research institute to study markets and develop products to fit these markets.

What are the implications of this development for U.S. agricultural trade? Should the United States seriously consider this area as a competitor or as a customer? Romania, Yugoslavia, and to some extent Bulgaria seem inclined to move farther afield than Western Europe. Romania is courting trade in cereals with Israel and other countries of the Middle East; Bulgaria does a prime cottonseed business with the Arab countries; both Romania and Bulgaria have received trade missions from Japan and are selling agricultural products to that country, mainly sunflower seeds in competition with U.S. soybeans.

While the Communist system of international trade has many hidden devices for manipulating values and undercutting world markets without reflections on paper, the dumping problem which results from subsidized exports in Western Europe presents a far more serious threat to U.S. agricultural trade than any anticipated dumping of low-priced agricultural items from Eastern Europe.

In the absence of a firm commercial trade policy by the EC, trade between the Eastern bloc and the Common Market and EFTA is bilateral and often involves outright barter. The barter method has been reduced to a minimum in recent years. Both Western European and Eastern European countries are finding more reasons for reestablishing trade on a more normal basis. Two countries in the EC (Germany and Italy) have shied away from any quick formation of a common commercial trade policy, largely because trade is being used as an instrument to establish political relations with the countries of the Danube basin. However, the latest survey by the Economic Commission for Europe points out that the Communist countries are now in the process of tech-

ıııʜııɡᴉ·ı ı̇ıᴗˈᴡᴗᴗᴡᴗᴡ, ꟷꟷʜꟷ Innovation, ꟷꟷ quality improvement. Overall growth rate targets were exceeded everywhere in 1968–
69, ranging from 6 percent in Poland and Hungary to 11 percent in
Bulgaria. The profit concept has been invoked in all countries as a
stimulus to improve technological levels, to assimilate output of technologically advanced goods, and to raise the quality of domestic output
to international standards. Price reform is bringing domestic prices
more in line with the international markets. Prior to 1966 prices had
little to do with the international market and were designed mainly to
fit into national and regional plans. For example, sulfuric acid—an
important item in many kinds of manufacture—is three and one-half
times more expensive in Russia than in France. Caustic soda is one and
one-half times more expensive in France than in Russia. The pricing
system employed by Russia is subject to adjustments based on political
plans or objectives of the moment. Under this bilateral bargaining on a
government-to-government basis, foreign trade has far less influence on
world prices than outright barter. Thus the satellite countries, smaller
and weaker at the negotiating table, find very definite drawbacks with
their Soviet-controlled trade policies. Trade negotiations rarely favor
the satellites, especially if results are compared with Russian trade in
countries outside the bloc. At the same time, imports of Russian
products to satellites cost an average of 38 percent more than the same
items sold in Western countries. With this system slowly but surely
breaking up, new opportunities appear for considerable expansion of
trade.

CHANGING U.S. POLICY

Adjustments in U.S. attitudes and laws are required before American agriculture and business can claim even the smallest portion of the
more than $10 billion East-West trade. Following President Johnson's
presentation of an East-West bill in 1967 considerable Congressional
activity was heavy on both sides of the issue. Hearings were held and a
ııʜıᴗ ꟷꟷıᴗˈı ᴗı ı̇ıᴗꟷᴗᴗᴗᴗ (ᴗᴗᴗᴗᴗᴗᴗꟷ ᴗᴗᴗ ᴗᴗᴗᴗᴗᴗᴗ) ᴗᴗᴗᴗᴗᴗ ᴗᴗᴗ ᴗᴗᴗᴗᴗᴗᴗᴗᴗ
ᴗᴗ legislation which would remove the many restrictions now imposed.
Preoccupation with the Vietnam War and opposition to granting credits
or establishing trade policy with any member of the Communist bloc
which supported the North Vietnamese slowed a major drive to pass
legislation. The same effort to improve trade was reflected in a speech
by Under Secretary of State Nicholas B. Katzenback shortly after
taking office in 1967, in which he urged abolition of the blockade of
U.S. trade with Eastern Europe: "Western trade is going to expand
with Eastern Communist countries, regardless of American limitation."
Katzenback called for abolishing most of the so-called strategic items
list (except for actual military equipment and armaments) and for an

end to the prohibition on trade which denied some Eastern European nations most-favored-nation treatment even though they are fellow members of the General Agreement on Tariffs and Trade (GATT). Hungary, Czechoslovakia, Poland, and Yugoslavia are signatories of GATT and thereby entitled to most-favored-nation treatment. But the United States extends most-favored-nation treatment only to Poland and Yugoslavia. This irks Czechoslovakia and Hungary, who argue that it prevents them from buying some U.S. agricultural items (cotton for example) since to do so would place them is unequal competition with Poland and Yugoslavia.

While the volume of trade in agriculture between Eastern Europe and the United States has been small, observations by this writer in the summer of 1967 clearly foreshadowed increased demand for several of the important export items of American agriculture. The list included cotton, feed grains, protein feeds (mostly soybeans), supplements for hog and poultry feeding, certain categories of agricultural inputs, small farm machinery, dairy equipment, and herbicides. Obviously certain U.S. restrictive trade policies would have to be modified if this market was to be reasonably attractive to U.S. exporters.

A special mission sent by USDA in the summer of 1968 reached a similar conclusion. In late 1972 a third agricultural trade survey was made by a special group of four, headed by Ray Ioanes, administrator of the Foreign Agriculture Service of USDA. The mission included representatives of the American Soybean Association, the Great Plains Wheat Association, and the U.S. Feed Grains Council. This team concluded that at least four of the six principal Eastern European countries were determined to improve the protein diets of their people in the years ahead, indicating increased use of feed grains, soybeans, and wheat to spur livestock production.

The 1968 trade mission concluded that two major obstacles were in the way of increased U.S. agricultural trade in this area:

1. U.S. unwillingness to allow the most-favored-nation treatment to Eastern European nations, even if they were GATT members.

2. The requirement that U.S. exporters sign an agreement that part of any grain cargo to Eastern Europe will be unloaded at a port other than in Eastern Europe. This raises shipping costs. Likewise, 50 percent of the cargoes financed under special credit arrangements must be carried in U.S. vessels, which charge much higher freight rates.

Feed grains, soybeans, cotton, wheat, and tobacco were listed as U.S. products which each of the six principal East European countries were interested in and were from time to time buying in small quantities through third-country channels. Rising living standards in the Eastern bloc and internal activity in small private sectors of industry and commurco have produced a demand for more variety and high-quality food, especially in the urban areas.

As matters stood in mid-1972 the issue of East-West trade, so far as the United States was concerned, was more a matter of international politics and domestic emotion than economics. Economically, the 4 percent of total world trade conducted by the six nations of the Eastern bloc is hardly worth the worry; yet it is important to a few firms and individuals in the United States.

The current U.S. policy toward Eastern Europe seems to encourage more trade efforts by the private sector and to hold out the prospect for major policy change pending settlement of some of the basic issues between the United States and Russia. As one relatively high government official concerned with trade remarked: "Nothing doing officially at the top level until the Vietnam War is settled, and that may take another ten years."

However, in spite of this pessimism, the administration in late 1970 and early 1971, slowly and without fanfare, was making significant moves to increase trade with the Eastern bloc. In 1970 Harold B. Scott, director of the Commerce Department's Bureau of International Commerce, made a survey of the Eastern European states. While acknowledging there were still barriers to major trade development—such as lack of most-favored-nation treatment, a psychological barrier among businessmen that too much activity with Eastern Europe would backfire against them in the United States, and lack of credit and export controls—Scott saw important opportunities for increased transfer of goods between the United States and the area. He argued that joint ventures now generally approved by the Eastern European states provided the best avenue for U.S. businessmen. This, said Scott, is "a way for the Eastern group to acquire both technology and management plus capital from the West."

There seems to be plenty of potential for trade if we look at what is happening at the present time. In 1968, for instance, Eastern European countries (excluding the Soviet Union) bought $2.7 billion worth of goods from the West. Of this amount $158 million came from the United States. The same nations sold $2.6 billion worth of goods to Western countries with $140 million of that going to the United States. The trade figure was up 30 percent overall in 1969, and at mid-1970 another increase of more than 20 percent was chalked up. The United States did not share proportionately in these increases.

Aside from the economic factor, which admittedly is not overwhelming for the United States, holding back may mean that we are losing more than just a limited business opportunity. The larger benefit relates to the continuing movement of these Eastern European countries away from the rigidities and ties of the recent past. Politically and economically, they are reasserting their national identities. The United States might well make a decision soon as to what policy will enhance this limited step toward improved relationships with the East and how to share more equitably in some of the international trade going to the West.[3]

---

3. Because of failure to reach an agreement between the United States and Soviet Russia on past-due war debts of Russia, the Export-Import Bank of the United States (set up in 1934 to finance export trade) had been prevented from assisting U.S. exporters in Russian trade. However, some 37 years later, Congress took under consideration legislation which would allow the Export-Import Bank to support U.S. imports to Russia. A later amendment extended this authority to Eastern Europe. This is expected to greatly facilitate trade with this area, especially in cotton, feed grains, and industrial goods. In mid-1972 Russia announced her willingness to begin negotiations to settle U.S. lend-lease war debts.

Chapter 14

ASSAULT ON NONTARIFF BARRIERS

EXCEPT IN SPECIAL CASES in particular industries, most observers of international trade agree that not much trade expansion can be expected from tariff reductions beyond what has resulted from the six rounds of tariff negotiations of the General Agreement on Tariffs and Trade (GATT) since World War II. With all the liberalization inherent in these negotiations, the growing use of devices other than tariff to protect various industries is of increasing concern to GATT members.

The European Community (EC) has been plagued with charges of restrictive practices. Recently, vigorous steps have been taken to reduce restrictions among the members. The move is toward common standards for manufactured goods such as textiles, safety devices on automobiles and tractors, and removal of a host of food processing regulations which make intrastate trade more difficult. Still to be tackled, however, are the external regulations such as variable levies (which the United States contends are nontariff barriers), special preferences, and quotas as well as the multitude of state trading, financing, and import restrictions which up to this point have been problems of the individual state rather than the Community. The only common uniform regulation affecting imports is the external tariff which was inaugurated before the end of the Kennedy Round in 1967.[1] One internal development which facilitates trade between the Six (but mostly concerns exporting coun-

---

1. The EC with a common external tariff is treated as a single state under GATT rules and subject to the same regulations of escape clauses which any member state of GATT may have. This was the basis on which the Israeli and Spanish special arrangements were made for the importation under quota and a preference of fresh citrus (see Chapter 11).

tries) is a new regulation eliminating border taxes and inaugurating a value-added tax on agricultural products in place of the cumulative turnover tax in force in some EC countries. This simply means that in each stage in agricultural production and distribution, only the actual net tax involved is passed on to the consumer. The main merit in the new system is that it will be uniform and easier to apply than the old system. It will afford little relief so far as actual taxes paid are concerned.

QUOTAS

In the broader sphere of international world trade a whole series of nontariff barriers are legal under GATT. The quota is by far the most widely used nontariff barrier. Quotas come under specific rules of GATT, and nations adopting them are subject to retaliation if they use them illegally and a member complains. Some negotiation officials doubt whether quotas can be abolished or reduced through periodic renegotiation of GATT. William Roth, special representative for trade negotiations under President Johnson, questioned "whether the nature of the nontariff barriers and the wide differences in the practices of different countries are such that over all nontariff barrier negotiations, conducted independently of a general round of trade negotiations, is a practical possibility of negotiating a code of uniform practices concerning the various categories of nontariff regulations." Others have suggested negotiation to establish "rules of competition," which might make the escape clauses and other legal devices under GATT more flexible and better understood. Something like this is practiced in the EC when, as happened during the French monetary crisis in 1968, France imposed special taxes and quotas against some intrastate trade as a temporary measure to protect the franc. This is permitted under the Rome Treaty, but the nation concerned must first notify the Commission and Council in Brussels of intended action and seek unanimous approval of such action. In a few cases such requested action by a member state has been denied, but generally the Council approves.

OTHER REGULATORS

The list of legal nontariff barriers or regulators of trade from an individual country or group of countries, such as EC, is formidable.

1. Quantitative restrictions. These may take the form of quotas (which limit the entry of certain goods into a country) or a complete embargo (as is often applied to seasonal crops which oversupply a local market at the peak of the local season). Quantitative restrictions are

used to some extent by virtually every Western trading country, including the EC and the United States. They are usually temporary and seasonal.

2. Variable levies and the gate price system. These devices are the chief methods of the EC for maintaining producer prices at what farmers in the Six regard as reasonable and fair levels. The word "fair" is widely used in all international trade negotiations and regulatory agencies; it has yet to be clearly defined.

3. Conditional imports. These result from mixing regulations. For instance, millers may be required to use only a certain percentage of imported grain to make flour. Devices making imports conditional on price level, volume of production, utilization, and other factors are also used. An example might be Turkish tobacco; a country may have a quota, but reduction of cigarette consumption or a change of blends might require the manufacturers in a given country to refuse to import Turkish tobacco up to the quota.

4. Monopolies. State or parastate trading agencies set up import goals or quotas and have state authority to determine whether imports of certain articles are to be allowed and what the conditions of entry will be.

5. Advance deposits on imports. By requiring higher or lower deposits for different countries, importing authorities can discriminate. An example is the United Kingdom's requirement that an importer deposit 50 percent of the value of the import six months before the goods are shipped.

6. Preferential treatment as to source of supply. This is a device widely used in Europe by countries desiring to establish special trade relations with another country or to trade in a nondollar area. It is often used by European and some Asian nations to save dollars for other purposes. For example, Austria forbids the import of American poultry and buys most of her poultry needs from Hungary because she has a favorable trade balance with Hungary and wants to continue to sell industrial products. This control is achieved through import licensing, by issuing private importers' licenses to import certain goods only if they come from a designated country.

7. Bilateral agreements and barter transactions. These often ignore actual prices entirely and are mere exchanges of goods at some agreed price level. Before World War II German potash interests and U.S. cotton traders exchanged products through barter agreements in which both potash and cotton were priced above the going dollar price in the world market. This device is now widely used by the Eastern European group and the Soviet Union.

All these devices are legal under present GATT rules. However, there are escape clauses and even provision for retaliation in case undue hardship results from legal trade restriction. The United States took advantage of the retaliation provision in the famous "chicken incident" when EC levies virtually eliminated U.S. poultry exports to EC countries. The United States invoked Article 23 of GATT, which permits retaliation, and increased the levies on German and French goods to pay for the loss in export revenue occasioned by EC's high levies on poultry.

MISCELLANEOUS DEVICES

In addition to these nontariff barriers which in certain circumstances are sanctioned by GATT, there are many new devices to circumvent the rules—health regulations, packaging standards, freight differentials, sanitary codes, and other measures a country can use to protect a sector of its economy. Since health, sanitary, and quality standards and freight rates are held to be the responsibility of each country, these can complicate the pattern of international trade.[2] Some health and sanitary regulations are purely arbitrary and designed more to protect a particular industry than to protect the consumers. For example, countries differ greatly in setting levels of tolerance for insecticides and antibiotics in food products. France forbids the import of poultry that has been fed some of the new antibiotics. France also has recently imposed a "safety" regulation on imported farm tractors which requires them to have headlights. Tariffs on tractors were reduced in the Kennedy Round by 2.5 percent; manufacturers said the cost of adding headlights offset the tariff cut, and thus the price of imported tractors remained about the same. Germany, a large exporter of tractors to France, protests. At the same time, German rules require all tractors coming into that country to have two sets of brakes and two seats. So it rapidly gets to a point of the pot calling the kettle black. Germany's level of tolerance for herbicide residuals in wheat and other food grains is very strict, much more so than in the United States. This virtually eliminates wheat from certain areas in the United States from the German market. Following the Kennedy Round, GATT produced a 276-page catalogue of the nontariff barriers then in existence. With the new wave of devices to circumvent GATT this list is already obsolete.

The hope is that the Common Market, which has committees at work on nontariff barriers that are primarily administrative and strictly national in nature, may come up with some rules. Agreement among EC nations would greatly simplify future negotiations, since the EC is the second largest market on the globe. Perhaps substantial progress has been made in this area, but there have also been ominous developments of concern to U.S. soybean producers (see Chapter 10). The EC has

---

2. The European Community's Transport Committee has developed, and the Council and Commission have approved, a Common Transport Policy covering road, rail, and inland waterway carriers of people and freight. Air and sea transport are excluded for the present because of the international nature of these services.

under consideration a vegetable oil tax of $60 per ton designed to discourage the purchase of soybeans as a source of cattle feed and margarine oil. Such a tax, say U.S. representatives, threatens soybean exports worth $500 million a year. Under the Kennedy Round soybeans
were bound to remain duty and quota free in the EC market. This internal tax may seriously offset the advantages which U.S. soybean producers received through GATT. United States tobacco, which also
gained an improved position under GATT, is being placed under the
Common Market levy system. While this development has created no
adverse trade problem yet, U.S. exporters see the possibility of losing
some of the $145 million market when Greece and Turkey, both important tobacco producers, are added to the Common Market as full
associate members. It is almost axiomatic that when the EC takes
control of a product, the producers of that product within the Community demand and get additional protection. This will encourage the
production of American-type tobacco within the present Six with oriental types coming from Greece and Turkey.

Price Support Systems

The price and income support systems in effect in various countries
including the United States and the subsidies to bring export prices
near the level of world prices can be nontariff barriers to trade. Except
in special cases production subsidies are outlawed in the EC; "fair
prices" under the market control and levy system, instead of subsidies,
are supposed to raise agricultural incomes to a level comparable with
those in the industrial sector. Outside the Community, and legal under
GATT, are numerous national support systems. In the United States
farmers are paid (in effect) not to produce certain crops, and in addition
U.S. farmers receive supported prices. Great Britain uses a system of
marketing boards through which supply is partially controlled; moreover, Britain directly subsidizes farmer unions. In the EC the "special
cases" excepted from the prohibition on subsidies are becoming more
numerous. Since the system used for establishing special cases is flexible
—subject only to the approval of the Commission (which is usually
given)—there have been enough such cases to produce considerable chaos
in world markets. In the summer of 1969 France sold 800,000 tons of
wheat to Communist China with an approved subsidy of $66.45 per ton.
This subsidy was higher than the cost of wheat in the world market.
The United States protested this sale on the grounds that it further demoralized the glutted international grain market.

No nation can escape some of the blame for these complicated restraints on trade. As one country takes some step to protect its producers and markets, it is likely that another nation which stands to lose
by the action will seek a way to subvert or retaliate against the action.

One might say, in fact, that "everybody does it." Unfortunately, no government is free enough or clean enough to act to take the lead in cutting back these numerous barriers. The best defense of the United States has been that we "do less of it than other countries."

U.S. PROTECTION

Basic protection for U.S. agricultural producers against undue outside competition was written into the original Agricultural Adjustment Act of 1933. According to Section 22 of that act the President has power, after due investigation by the tariff commission, to impose fees on imported agricultural commodities if they seriously interfere with domestic price support programs. Under this provision import restrictions are imposed on wheat, wheat products, cotton, peanuts, butter, certain cheese, and other dairy products. The Sugar Act of 1948, as amended, provides a formula for dividing the U.S. market (by quotas) between U.S. and foreign suppliers. The Meat Import Act of 1964 authorizes the President to limit imports of fresh, chilled, or frozen beef, sheep, and goat meat. There is also a fur embargo on imports of ermine, fox, kilinsky, marten, mink, muskrat, weasel, and other fur skins from the Soviet Union and Communist China. As an added protection to U.S. producers, based on the tariff act of 1930, the Treasury Department may impose countervailing duties when a dutiable import is benefiting from a bounty or grant. In addition we have the "Buy American Act," which requires that defense and foreign aid procurement funds must be spent for domestically produced products. All this, argue other countries, is trade discrimination.

The Trade Expansion Act of 1962 gave a new tool to the U.S. President in handling discriminatory practices. Section 252 of the act provides that where a foreign country engages in discriminatory acts or policies which unjustifiably restrict U.S. commerce, the United States may take remedial tariff action—that is, suspend preferences, increase tariffs, or apply countervailing duties. The countervailing duty system, long used in the United States, is essentially the same as the levy system in the EC, except that the variable levy as used by the EC is much less cumbersome to apply and almost instantly effective when the Commission approves the levy. In the United States the countervailing tariffs can be used only when harm to a domestic industry is proven before the U.S. Tariff Commission.

Roth, in his final report to President Johnson in 1968, argued that Section 252 of the Trade Expansion Act of 1962 should be amended "to permit the full range of retaliatory power to be available in accordance with GATT."

United States health and sanitary regulations, in the view of some international traders, are discriminatory and barriers to trade, even as we argue that similar regulations of European countries are effective against U.S products. For example, sanitary regulations in the 1903 tariff forbid the importation of any meat product from a country where foot-and-mouth disease exists. In other cases, standards of wholesomeness required of imports are based on U.S. domestic standards which sometimes are designed to manipulate the market rather than protect health. A case involving imports of Gorgonzola cheese from Italy just after World War II will illustrate. For years Gorgonzola cheese had been a highly sought after specialty cheese. During World War II imports of Gorgonzola were cut off and the industry was virtually eliminated by the Germans and the Italians who used the milk and the cattle for immediate food consumption. After the war this industry was revived through efforts of the U.S. military government in Italy and the farmers in the Po Valley. During the war two or three small firms in the United States had learned to produce a type of cheese similar to Gorgonzola, and after the war these firms naturally wanted protection for their industry. When their protests to the U.S. Tariff Commission and the USDA brought no results, they asked the U.S. Public Health Service to study the "foreign matter" in Italian Gorgonzola cheese. Although this cheese had been coming into the United States for years with no challenge or detriment to the health of U.S. consumers, now the Health Service contended that the foreign matter constituted a violation of U.S. standards, and the importation of the cheese was stopped. Only after much diplomatic activity and a careful scrutiny of the Italian cheese-making plants by U.S. agricultural attachés was importation of the cheese resumed. In similarly absurd regulations the United States prohibits the use of any fish oil in the production of margarine, although most countries of the world blend herring oil with vegetable oils in this product. Other regulations under the Wholesome Meat Act requiring special packaging and labeling, argue some foreign producers, are barriers.

EFFECTS

One measure of determining the worst offenders in the use of these nontariff barriers might be the percentage of total international trade in each country that is covered by one or more of these devices. As early as 1963 the USDA made an extensive study of the nontariff trade barriers which seventeen countries representing nearly 80 percent of all international trade in agricultural products used to protect the agricultural sector of their economies. It is admitted by all that the nontariff barriers do not mean a country does not trade. Indeed, some of the countries having the strictest regulations have a high volume of trade. Nontariff barriers do mean that trade becomes difficult and the barriers cannot be reconciled with the ideal of a free movement of goods. They hamper movement (particularly of food) and are incompatible with efficiency, with an international division of labor, and with the most economical use of resources. Percentages of total agricultural production in each country under some sort of nontariff controls, as revealed by the 1963 USDA study, are shown in Table 14.1.

TABLE 14.1

United States	26	Japan	76	France	94
United Kingdom	37	Netherlands	79	Switzerland	94
Canada	41	Greece	82	Norway	97
Australia	41	Denmark	87	New Zealand	100
Italy	63	Austria	91	Portugal	100
Belgium	76	West Germany	93		

It does not necessarily follow from an examination of these statistics that total international agricultural trade would be materially increased if most or all of these barriers were removed. It would result in a major reallocation of resources devoted to some crops. It would greatly increase the exports of the United States and one or two other countries, but such a radical adjustment would have political and social repercussions far beyond the benefits of liberalized trade.

The USDA recognized this fact at the time the 1963 report on nontariff barriers became public. Secretary Freeman said: "As realists, we are not seeking completely free trade. For many reasons—economic, political and social—no country is either prepared or willing to remove all protections from its agriculture. The basic issue is the degree of protection."

More recent data show an increase in the amount of U.S. trade covered by regulations outside the tariff structure, and increases are also shown for some other countries. However, in the case of the EC countries, barriers among themselves are virtually eliminated. Once the nations of the Common Market agreed on a uniform external tariff system, many of the nontariff barriers formerly used by the individual countries were employed by the EC as a whole. This factor, along with the system of market control by the EC itself, caused grave concern to all outside countries which had formerly supplied the Six individually. The USDA, in a recent study of the effects of the creation of the Common Market on U.S. international trade in agricultural products, commented as follows:

The Common Agricultural Policy has introduced major changes in agricultural market for many agricultural commodities. The high levels to support farm income, combined with efforts to insulate the community from world markets, have placed much of the community import system in a category which is not amenable to normal tariff negotiations. The high internal prices tend to encourage increases in production while dampening the growth of consumption. The freeing of international trade and the application of variable levies to imports relegates the United States and other exporting countries outside the community to residual suppliers because they are not permitted to compete with the EC on a price basis.

Another effect of EC policy is that the United States, Canada, Argentina, Denmark, and other agricultural exporters turn to other markets and compete with each other outside the Community at the same time that the EC—with surpluses mounting in several products (chiefly dairy, soft wheat, poultry, and sugar)—subsidizes these exports into third-country outlets, and the wheel keeps turning toward what might well become a subsidy war.

AGRICULTURE UNDER GATT

Agriculture may well be the most difficult issue to handle in any future trade negotiations under GATT. As early as 1967 the Ministers of the Contracting Parties—the 76 nations belonging to GATT—formed an Agricultural Committee to "examine the problems in the agricultural sector."

The Committee, meeting in January 1968, set up a three-stage work program:

1. Documentation to clarify the position of agricultural trade in about eight of the principal temperate zone agricultural products moving in international trade.

2. Identification of problems and conditions affecting international trade in these products.

3. Finding mutually acceptable solutions to the problems identified.

Stages one and two of the Committee's work program had been completed by fall 1969. At the first meeting of the Committee after completion of stage two, the United States argued that (a) high support prices, (b) uneconomic production, (c) artificial export pricing practices, and (d) import protection were the principal problems in agriculture and should have priority attention. This view seems to have been generally shared by the other contracting parties except the representatives of EC, who contended that this narrow economic view skirted the human issues in agriculture and the necessity to provide the rural sector with living standards and income closer to urban standards. The Committee did not reach agreement in 1969 on solutions to the four problem areas outlined by the United States.

Representatives of GATT met in Geneva in February 1970 for a general review of the work of various committees and to consider possibilities of a round of negotiations in 1972 on nontariff barriers. No decision was reached about a 1972 negotiation session since the delegates can only discuss and recommend; contracting governments must decide matters of substance. Subcommittees on support prices, uneconomic production, export pricing policies, and import protection had been set up by a previous session. Little progress was reported because of the wide divergence of opinion and practice by individual countries on the major problems. However, in the closing sessions Henry Brodie, the U.S. representative, proposed that GATT adopt a "declaration of intent" in which each member would pledge not to introduce new measures hampering the flow of trade and not to reinforce existing ones. But Brodie's effort was nullified by the furor in Europe and America over the Trade Bill of 1970 then under consideration in Congress, which, among its provisions, made stronger the utilization of quotas and other devices to protect some seventy segments of U.S. industry.

An informal meeting of the contracting parties was held in Geneva in April 1971 where agricultural trade again held the center of attention. Various committees reported informally; after a lengthy review of the rather bleak outlook for accomplishing any major breakthrough on nontariff barriers, Carl J. Gilbert, special representative for U.S. trade negotiations, suggested: "On our part we are coming to realize that the coordination of agricultural policies and the improvement of trading rules must go together. Otherwise, it will be hard to negotiate obligations under GATT that can be maintained."

In the maneuvers and negotiations between the United States and the Common Market early in 1972 dealing with the removal of the American imposed 10 percent surcharge on imports and the overall revaluation of the dollar, there appears to have been some agreement to take up the question of nontariff barriers sometime in 1973. The United States has steadily insisted on an early discussion of this problem while the Common Market countries have resisted early action. On the other hand, the Common Market countries have insisted on some version of the Second Mansholt Plan—that is, worldwide commodity agreements— to stabilize world prices. The United States has agreed to discuss this issue as part of the proposed negotiations in GATT late in 1973.

Chapter 15

A NEW THRESHOLD

THE HISTORIC 1969 DECISION by the Council of Ministers at the Hague to enlarge the Common Market—followed by the successful negotiations between the Six and Great Britain for her admission—shifted the emphasis from the everyday operational problems to economic integration, common currency, and some form of political unity. This was observed in the Pompidou-Heath talks, and, preceding the accession agreement, leaders of other members of the Community spoke of the necessity for some sort of political body which would reflect a consensus on world-wide political issues. The Commission at Brussels has long urged this development. Franco Maria Malfatti (the Commission President who took office July 2, 1970)[1] in a major policy address in Hanover in April 1971 said: "The international situation and internal requirements and political will of our people alike demand that Europe should finally take the plunge of political unity."

Whether this political unification will come quickly or develop over the next quarter-century, one must be impressed by the performance of the Common Market area economically between its founding in 1958 and the landmark decision at the Hague in 1969.

Three basic objectives were spelled out in the Treaty of Rome which created the Common Market: (1) a customs union, permitting free movement of goods and people between the member states; (2) integration of the economies with uniform fiscal, transportation, labor,

1. Malfatti resigned as President of the Commission in early 1972 to return to Italy and enter politics. Under the rotation system France will chair the Commission in 1973.

social security, and business laws; (3) political unity along the lines of a superstate or a federation with a common foreign policy, defense establishment, fiscal system, and development policy. The treaty provided for the creation of institutions to carry out these objectives over a period of time. The ten-year transition period established by the founders to effect the customs union and some of the economic integration ended December 31, 1969.

ACHIEVEMENTS

The first of the three goals—a customs union—was achieved by June 30, 1968, when tariff walls of the six members of the Common Market came down. In fact, by 1968 something more than a mere customs union had been achieved; an external tariff had been established, and a single individual spoke for all the Market countries in international tariff negotiations. A Common Agricultural Policy, after nearly eight years of sometimes bitter and disruptive negotiations, was a reality. Movement of goods, persons, and even visitors from outside the Six was freed of many of the formalities, visas, inspections, and roadblocks common to Europe in an earlier day. A mass market of some 185 million people had been created. There had been considerable rationalization of the transportation system of the Six by January 1, 1970. In addition to the elaborate railway, airline, and barge systems, an integrated network of superhighways was under plan and/or construction in each country. A common energy resource system was in the making; agreement had been reached on financing agriculture; and enlargement of the Community was in progress.

GOALS

Fiscal integration or some form of a common currency is yet to come. The kind of political structure that will eventually rise over this economic structure is one of the question marks of the long future.

The dream of postwar Europe's senior statesmen that some sort of political unity might evolve was not in sight when the tariff barriers came down in June 1968; nor was there a serious prospect for political union on the settlement of the thorny issue of financing agriculture and enlargement of the market. However, the meeting of the Council of Ministers at the Hague cleared the way for enlargement of the market and provided a formula for financing agriculture. The discussions in May 1971 between Heath and Pompidou seemed to point to some sort of understanding on the type of European unity which will be sought in the future.

Europe, coming out of World War II, had to act collectively to surιίιιι, ιΙιι ριιιιΙιιιιι ΙιιιιιΙιιιιι ΙιιιιΙ ΙιιιμιιιΙ ιιι ιιιΙιιιιι ιιιιιιιιιιιιι, ριιιΙιιΙιιιιιΙ, ιιιιιΙ social structures which would truly effect some sort of a United States of Europe. Postwar prosperity, the unclear stalemate between the Soviet Union and United States and the umbrella which this afforded, growing concern with internal problems, disillusionment of youth with the old order, and the rise of younger leaders who were soldiers rather than policy makers in World War II shifted attention away from inter-nationalism and outer world affairs. There was more concern for gaining a foothold in the affluence the postwar boom produced. The challenge to integrate politically seemed less vital as the real war dangers from the East subsided and as each nation looked more and more to its internal problems. The urge for some greater political unity and the super power state probably was only something to speculate upon.

Steps to rationalize the corporate laws and regulations in each country dealing with mergers and free movement of investment capital have been taken. The Council of Ministers approved late in 1964 a convention on corporate law. In preparation since 1962, the docu-ment required each country to recognize companies and corporate bodies. Thus a company headquartered in one of the nations of the Common Market will normally receive automatic recognition by the government and courts of all other Common Market countries. This action is expected to facilitate the growth of larger companies operating throughout the customs union. Three major corporate mergers already have been achieved. One came in 1967 when Germany's Agfa and Bel-gium's Gervart film and camera companies merged. The second was the merger of Citroen, an old established French automobile firm, with Fiat of Italy. Recently a union of textile companies, spread over three countries and 400 production and retail units, was completed. In early 1970 the Commission approved a reciprocal manufacturing arrange-ment between Dunlop Tires of France and Pirelli of Italy which was, in effect, a merger of their sales and distribution systems. The Commis-sion also approved the merger of twenty-three coal companies in the Ruhr, making one of the largest coal combines on the Continent.

ROLE OF AGRICULTURE

Agriculture still is of almost continual concern to all nations of the Common Market. As the same time, it has emerged as the sector in the whole market structure which is truly integrated and institutionalized. Although the outlook for agriculture is bright, many troublesome issues lie ahead for the ministers to ponder. The Common Agricultural Policy, which from the beginning has protected the producer from lower-cost imports with resulting high prices and higher income, has at the same time brought on towering surpluses of almost everything in temperate zone farm products except beef and veal. The cost of handling these surpluses and of disposing of them in the world market has long since absorbed all the funds acquired through the levies on imports. For the first time since the creation of the Common Market the finance ministers met with the agricultural ministers in Brussels in midsummer 1969 in an effort to reduce the costs of handling surpluses or to devise a long-term plan to balance production with local and international potential markets.

Aside from the troublesome problems of monetary reform, agricultural surpluses, and treasury drains for export subsidies, other issues call for continuous adjustment. There are no tariff barriers to intra-community trade, but quotas, packing and sanitary regulations, import taxes, and numerous small technical regulations peculiar to each country are even more effective than tariffs in discouraging trade. A common transportation policy is in the making, but the manipulation of freight rates by a national railroad can be as effective in slowing down distribution of goods as tariffs or quotas. A common policy on competition in the Market is still to be adopted. Common social, financial, and welfare policies are a must in the decade ahead if true economic integration is to be achieved.

Trade with Eastern Europe

The Rome Treaty stipulated that the question of trade relations with Eastern Europe be resolved by 1970; this has been postponed until 1973. In 1971 the Six were still divided on this issue. The smaller states of Belgium, Luxembourg, Holland, and Italy inclined toward a common trade policy which would apply to the countries of the Eastern bloc as it would to all other countries outside the Common Market. Germany and France preferred the "special arrangement" which, in effect, is a barter between the Community and a state of the Eastern bloc. Beginning in 1970 these "special bilateral arrangements" had to be negotiated by the Commission and approved by the Council. In practice the one of the Six most interested in the transaction negotiates the trade, subject to overall guidelines and approval by the Council.

However, in late 1969 a small step toward an overall common trade policy with the Eastern bloc was agreed on which will modify to some extent the practice of recent years. The new rules adopted by the Six stipulate that no member state will unilaterally impose quotas or restrictions on the series of products appearing on "liberation lists." This enables some 400 items from the six principal East European states to enter on a quota-free basis. For the Soviet Union, however, the list includes only forty tariff positions.

The technical gap

For years Europe has talked about the technical gap between individual European states and the United States. Although international committees are at work on the problem, each country seems determined to develop technological sophistication on a national rather than an international basis. Whether or not Europeans adopt national or international methods, attitudes and courses will have to be changed in their educational systems. To many persons the European educational systems seem out of date and inadequate for the age of mechanics and science. There are, for instance, only twenty-three universities in all of France. The Common Market countries with 185 million people turn out about 100,000 university graduates per year—most of them in law, medicine, and liberal arts. Only one university in France and no more than one or two in Germany really gives attention to technical agriculture. The United States with more than 209 million population produces some 450,000 college graduates per year, a high percentage of them in the sciences and technological fields. Russia with 235 million persons produces 345,000 graduates per year, most of which are in the scientific disciplines.

As one step toward closing the technological gap and broadening the area of cooperation with other countries in Europe, the Community early in 1969 issued a prospectus for a new "technological community." Based on the Euratom–Coal and Steel Community pattern, outside countries such as Britain and the Scandinavian countries could participate without total membership in the Common Market. France, which has opposed unification, is supporting the new technological community plan. Late in 1970 the idea of a European or Community University was revived. The next steps undoubtedly will be slow and at times painful for some of the members, and the problems at present are enormous. Nonetheless, the success of economic integration discounts any small setbacks which have occurred or may occur in the future.

Progress and Problems

Jean Rey, President of the Commission of European Communities in 1969, noted in his general report to the European Parliament in March of that year that during the transition period the Community had, for all practical purposes, attained its objectives in the customs field with regard to the movement of farm products and workers. It was quite obvious, he pointed out, that "we are behind schedule in other spheres, such as nongovernmental monopolies and freedom of establishment." In his extended report Rey suggested drawing up a work program, with priorities and a timetable, for the next three to five years. He called for an end to the postponement of decisions about Common Agricultural Policy, finance, and surplus disposal.

Three problems demanded attention, according to President Rey: (1) extension of market organizations to wine, tobacco, and fisheries; (2) establishment of definite financial regulations pertaining to agriculture—that is, resolution of formulas for contributing to the Guarantee and Guidance Fund and other fiscal responsibilities (agreement in principle was reached in late 1969 and early 1970); (3) the whole range of structural problems, balanced conditions in the various markets, and industrial and foreign trade policy.

The final part of Rey's statement dealt with enlargement of the Community, relations with the United States and the signatories of the Yaounde Convention, and settlement of relations with Great Britain. To deny Great Britain admission to the Community did not, in Rey's view, solve the problem of British relations. Since Great Britain was bound by many ties to the Continent, trouble for the British pound meant trouble for the Community. When Great Britain undertook to solve her fiscal difficulties with a 15 percent surtax, it affected the Community. On the question of relations with the United States, Rey recalled that President Nixon during his visit in January 1969 expressed concern over the Community's "highly protectionist external trade policy and the use of subsidies to in effect make war on the United States in third-country markets."

Most of the issues raised by Rey in 1969 are on the way to some solution. Others of them—nontariff barriers between the Community and the outside, rationalization of internal product standards, and the necessity for some sort of a stronger central authority—keep in the forefront the touchy question of how much political cooperation will be required.

Commission President Malfatti was able to report in his review in 1971 substantial progress in most of the issues outlined by his predecessor. The Hague summit conference had reaffirmed its determination to develop monetary cooperation on the basis of harmonized economic policies. In 1970 the Community activated a $2 billion reserve pool to provide short-term monetary help for a member state in difficulties. The states will consult each other before taking independent economic policy decisions. In 1971 the Six had launched a three-stage plan for economic and monetary union. This plan provides for continuous consultation on monetary matters and narrows the fluctuations between the currencies of the Six. By the end of 1973 major political decisions will be made on the ultimate nature of the union.

Malfatti could also report that the Community was now the world's largest trading power for intracommunity imports and exports. He noted that the Community was investing a greater portion of its gross national product in assistance to developing countries than the United

States. With an obvious reference to the mounting criticism in the United States of the Community's protective policies, he pointed out that American investment in the Community has increased fivefold since 1958; that the United States has had an average trade surplus with the Community of $2 billion a year since 1958. He concluded with an assertion that the Community and the United States represented 38 percent of all international trade and that "we could not forget the particular responsibility that the Community and the United States have in promoting freedom of trade."

The internal and external pressures on the Six, both economic and political, may well be a catalyst which will force more political unity than now seems possible or probable. As one wise and rising young leader remarked in the summer of 1968: "There is truly too much at stake to turn back now. We must depend on our intelligence and persistence to meet the problems which the Market has helped to create. There is no other way to go than forward."

Chapter 16

IMPLICATIONS OF THE ENLARGED COMMON MARKET

IN MID-1971—after ten years of advance and retreat, reams of white paper, much diplomatic shifting of position, and some honest soul-searching—Great Britain and three of her partners in the European Free Trade Association (EFTA) were in the final stages of formal membership in the Common Market by early 1973. In the wings awaiting some sort of less formal and binding association were four other EFTA partners—Austria, Switzerland, Sweden, and Portugal.

The chief obstacles to British entry between the first application in 1961–62 and the developments in 1969–70 that brought the various parties together in principle had been British reluctance to scuttle her low-price import policy on agricultural products and the unacceptable preconditions imposed by France. Most of the French preconditions were eliminated or modified at the meeting of the Council of Ministers of the Common Market at the Hague in December 1969. There a resolution was passed providing for the beginning of negotiations with Great Britain, Denmark, Ireland, and Norway by June 1970. Only after France had exacted a pledge that a permanent farm financing system would be made firm by the end of 1970 did the resolution unanimously carry. France had argued for the continuation of the system then in use, which allowed her to benefit most from the levies on imported agricultural products. The final communique, said to have been written by France's President Georges Pompidou, pledged the Common Market members to prepare and participate in the negotiations with Great Britain in the most "positive spirit." The communique also warned that something would have to be done about the Community's expanding farm surpluses. At an earlier historic session of the Council of Ministers at Brussels some of the unresolved problems were attacked. This was in a stop-the-clock session on December 29, 1969, when two of the basic issues—enlargement of the Common Market and a permanent financing system for agriculture—were resolved. This meeting also set a target date of 1980 for the integration and development of a common currency or fiscal system. In a formal visit to Great Britain early in 1970, Pompidou remarked that "British entry is now not a question but a matter of when agreement and negotiations could be completed for a full membership."

The agreement on financing agriculture was of special concern to France and Germany. Over the past years the levies on imported agricultural products were not sufficient to take care of the mounting costs of supporting prices and disposing of surplus agricultural products. In 1969 Germany contributed some $324 million to the Guarantee and Guidance Fund and France received out of the fund some $343 million for handling its surpluses and exporting its agricultural products. The agreement provided that from 1970 to 1975 the Guarantee and Guidance Fund would be supplemented by direct contributions from the budgets of each of the six countries in order to keep the fund at a level of about $3 billion per year. After 1975 all agricultural levies and industrial customs duties plus certain sales or value-added taxes will be placed in a common pool, and the direct contributions from each state budget will be diminished or eliminated.

CONDITIONS OF MEMBERSHIP

The principal applicants for membership in the Community agreed to accept the institutions, policies, and regulations of the Six as they stood. Early in 1970 representatives of the four met with the Commission in Brussels for a briefing on the implications of their acceptance and the position the Six would take at the beginning of membership negotiations. Formal discussions began on schedule, June 30, 1970. Denmark seemed willing to sign into membership with little or no preliminary discussions. Norway, while anxious to move quickly, was concerned that her fisheries industry might be adversely affected by too rapid a change. Ireland, along with Great Britain, had many problems and concerns, not the least of which was public opinion. British public opinion polls in mid-1970 showed less than 20 percent of the British populace in favor of joining the Common Market. A similar poll in 1961 had shown 70 percent in favor of joining.

Four issues had to be resolved in principle before negotiations with the British could begin on specific terms. First and foremost was length and nature of the transition period during which Great Britain would adjust her industry and agriculture to the regulations and policies of the Common Market. Second was the amount of Britain's contribution to the Guarantee and Guidance Fund from the import levies collected against agricultural products. Of major concern also was the increased cost of food to British consumers which would result from the higher levies. As the largest importer of food in the enlarged organization she would collect the most in the form of levies against imports; as a result of these levies, her consumers would pay a higher price for the food products. The other issues were the timing of monetary reform and the kind of economic and political integration planned for the longer future.

On December 8, 1970, the length of the transition period for industry and agriculture was set at five years. Britain previously had insisted on five for industry and eight for agriculture, but she agreed to adjust to the Community's financial arrangements in five years. The Six assured Britain that she would not pay a disproportionate amount into the Guarantee and Guidance Fund. West Germany, presently the highest contributor to the fund and also somewhat unhappy at the amount she gets back from the fund for the modernization of her agricultural production and marketing structure, strongly supported the idea of a pledge against disproportionate assessments. Britain was apprehensive about the drives for complete monetary reform by 1980 and reconstructing European agriculture over the next ten to twenty years. However, discussions did not reach a critical stage on these issues since they were obviously long-time programs. The Council of Ministers in a later session relieved the worries of the new applicants by refusing to approve Luxembourg Prime Minister Pierre Werner's proposal for an economic and monetary union by 1980. The Council of Ministers also turned down the Mansholt plan for structural reform in agriculture. Initial steps in both these plans, if the Commission's views had been followed, would have been undertaken during 1971 (see Chapter 17 for details).

The Werner finance plan included requirements that would have been difficult for France to accept, not to mention Britain: (1) Community currencies to be given irrevocable and immediate fixed parity one with the other. (Presently they vary according to world fiscal markets.); (2) credit and fiscal policies to be centralized in the Community; (3) a common monetary policy toward the rest of the world to be agreed upon; (4) all main components of national budget policies to be decided upon at the Community level instead of the national level; (5) introduction before 1980 of a common currency.

Acceptance of this plan clearly would have been an important move in the direction of central government for the Community. It also would have been a major obstacle to enlarging the Market, then or in the near future. Since the ideas seemed as unacceptable to some members of the Six as to the prospective new members, the issue was deferred for later consideration.

As on so many issues over the years, a compromise was reached at the

February 1971 meeting of the Council on a plan to move toward economic and monetary union and a common currency by 1980. The agreement does not make Europe a unitary state or a union of nation states. The move toward a common currency is to be taken in two stages. The first stage, ending in 1973 and coinciding with formal British membership, calls for a closer coordination of monetary policies and narrowing of the margins between the currencies of the Six. The second stage, which runs from 1973 to 1975, provides for the Council of Ministers—on the basis of proposals from the European Economic Commission—to decide how to move toward a centralized banking system and integrated currencies.

APPLICATION OF REGULATIONS

With most of the principles settled, formal talks began in mid-1971 to work out detailed application of the regulations and institutional operations of the Community to Great Britain and her partners. Foremost in the minds of the British negotiators (aside from the very large issue of the kind of European Union likely to emerge over the years ahead) was the cost to British consumers. Foremost in the minds of leaders of nations outside the Community, particularly the food-exporting countries, was the effect of British membership on the lucrative export market in Britain. Many studies have been made inside and outside Great Britain on this issue. That the low-price import policy and compensatory subsidies to her agricultural producers will have to change during the transition period is without question.

GREAT BRITAIN

On Britain's contribution to the Guarantee and Guidance Fund the negotiations started far apart, but both sides publicly expressed confidence that this issue was a matter of detail and would be resolved in due course. Higher consumer costs in Britain was the political issue which the Conservative government had to resolve. While Britishers argue that their country is giving up her sovereignty, a large part of the rising opposition in 1970 and 1971 to joining the Market seemed to be a part of the consumer revolt against the threat of higher food prices.

Britain's powerful Farmer's Union has consistently pointed out that if British farmers are to have anything near equal incomes with urban workers and if national policy continues to support importing low-cost food, they must have payments from the treasury. If farm subsidies ceased but taxes on food imports increased, the consumer would have to pay more for all foods. As early as the summer of 1968 agricultural ministry officials told this writer that pressure on the national budget and other political considerations simply meant that sooner or later, whether Britain joined the Community or not, farm subsidies would have to come down and more of the farm income would have to come from the marketplace. The Heath government in 1970 took initial steps by raising import taxes and reducing some of the subsidies to agriculture. This was regarded as a move toward the equalization that will have to come. Meanwhile, British industry seemed to be tooling up with full confidence that membership would mean increased business. British industry along with industries based in the United States and other countries are rushing behind the Community wall in joint ventures and outright purchase of industrial enterprises in the Community. Statistics in 1970 showed that between 1961 and 1969 non-Community countries acquired 820 companies within the Common Market. Only 215 companies within the Market purchased holdings outside. During the same period 1,000 joint ventures of various kinds were created among companies within the Community and 2,979 mergers or ventures with concerns outside the area.

The price Britain will have to pay for membership revolved around three items: (1) the higher price British consumers have to pay because of levies, (2) the amount of money required for the Community budget and the Guarantee and Guidance Fund, and (3) the effect of all this on the British balance of payments resulting from higher food import prices. In 1966–67 a British White Paper estimated that if Britain entered under present rules and prices the annual cost would be $490 million. A study by the Farmer's Union set the cost at $700 million. These figures are disputed by some economists. A figure not in excess of the average of the two estimates—about $580 million—is the limit. Equally varied estimates were made on actual food cost, although it was generally agreed food costs would rise.

The government White Paper estimates food costs will rise by 10–14 percent, an increase in the cost of living index of between 2.5 and 3.5 percent. This estimate takes into account that cereals and some other food imports such as mutton, beef, lamb, eggs, sugar, and butter would be higher. Some fruits and vegetable items would be lower. Assuming present world prices, no major change in levies by the EC, and increased cost of home-produced food, the Farmer's Union estimates consumers would pay as much as $940 million more for food—an overall rise in the consumer's total expenditure for food of 6 percent. However, the Union admits that with the abolition of subsidies to domestic producers there will be a tax saving to the treasury of $654 million. If this tax saving is passed on to the consumer, the actual increase will be only 1.6 percent. Most British authorities in touch with the day-to-day operations of the British system argue that adjustments can and will be made in agriculture which will be beneficial. The free entry of British capital, industrial goods, technology, and trade into this ten-nation area and increasing number of associate states will offset any losses that will occur in the agricultural sector.

In the initial diplomatic skirmishing over the amount Great Britain will pay into the Community budget and the Guarantee and Guidance Fund, Britain's limit had been set at $72 million in the expected year of admission, 1973; it will build gradually to around $450 million by the end of the five-year transition period in 1978. This was about half the amount some authorities estimated Britain would pay if costs were allocated under the present formula. While each country puts something into the Community budget and takes something out, Germany and Britain as the largest importers with smaller farm industries take out much less than the others. Under the formula Britain proposed, her part of the Community's total budget would be 12–15 percent. The six-nation community was thinking in terms of 20–22 percent for Great Britain.[1]

BRITISH COMMONWEALTH

The effects of British membership on the Commonwealth have not entered large in the current discussions. Presumably arrangements will be worked out during the transition period for agriculture and industry. The most important changes will be with regard to the British preferences now in force for Commonwealth agricultural products and preferential industrial arrangements for Britain in the Commonwealth. The Commonwealth partner with the most to lose is New Zealand, although Australia is concerned about declining wheat exports to Britain. The Commission in Brussels predicted that when Britain entered the Community, New Zealand's butter exports to the new Community would be cut in half. This would mean 90,000 tons of surplus butter New Zealand would need to dispose of in other markets. This figure was termed "quite unacceptable" by New Zealand.[2] The British position was that New Zealand should be allowed to sell its full quota of butter to Great Britain over the five-year transition period and in the sixth year a review would be made and adjustments of imports from New Zealand would be agreed upon. In terms of global trade, the economic effects of cutting off New Zealand butter from the Community would not be staggering (an estimated $80–180 million a year). However, to a small agricultural country with only 3 million people this loss would be serious. Canada and Australia, major shippers of wheat to Britain, also would suffer. However, both of these countries are shifting their sales efforts to the Orient and have already penetrated the Chinese and Japanese markets.

---

1. See Chapter 6. The figure agreed to in the final round of negotiations to be reached in stages by 1978 was 19.19 percent.

2. The special arrangement finally agreed to in the negotiations gives New Zealand a guaranteed market in the Community for 136,000 tons of butter and 15,000 tons of cheese. A review of the situation in 1977 is provided for to insure special arrangements beyond that period.

DENMARK

Of the three British partners now formal associate members of the Community, probably Denmark is the country that benefits the most initially. Trade arrangements tie Denmark's agricultural exports closely to the British market—particularly her pork, dairy, and poultry products. Denmark has increased her agricultural exports to the EC by 70 percent since 1963 and to EFTA by 40 percent. Despite these advances, expanding production year by year has kept Denmark smothered in agricultural surpluses. With competition from the EC in third-country markets and the necessity to surmount high levies raised by the EC, Denmark has resorted to all sorts of devices to keep her agricultural products moving. Three years ago a two-price system was inaugurated whereby high taxes and fixed prices were introduced on the home front in order to provide the subsidies to meet the export competition. Danish trade balance had been declining drastically since 1963, reaching an all-time high of $420 million in 1969. The balance of payments accounting for deficits all along the line was nearly one and one-half times this amount ($640 million) in 1960. In the summer of 1968 this writer visited Denmark and talked to officers of the ministries of agriculture, foreign trade, economics, and commerce as well as the principal leaders of the large cooperatives responsible for most of Denmark's agricultural export. To a man they were anxious to join the European Community but felt that Britain would have to be admitted first in order that they might preserve some, if not all, of their preferential position in the British market. There appeared to be little concern over the fact that the Community already produced surpluses of many of the products Denmark traditionally exports. The main concern was to find protection beneath the price umbrella of the Community and also to tap the Guarantee and Guidance Fund for subsidies to Danish products in third-country markets. Denmark accepted the Community's institutions and policies without question and was ready to join at any time the British entry was concluded. As the Danish Minister of Economics remarked following the briefings in Brussels in the summer of 1970, "Denmark's biggest problems are other people's problems. We are ready to join now."

IRELAND

The Irish Republic, closely tied to Britain economically and with some of the same agricultural problems as Denmark and some possible initial industrial adjustments to make on assembly plants, also felt that Ireland can "join immediately, without tears."

NORWAY

Norway, the fourth member to seek associate membership, had strong political opposition in some quarters and was apprehensive about

what open competition within the Community would do to her small
agricultural economy and how her fishery industries would profit under
the new fisheries policy that went into effect February 1, 1971. Norway's
agricultural output represents only about 1 percent of the total agricultural production of the enlarged Community, and she argued for an
exemption from the Common Agricultural Policy. Norway produces
six times the fish products of the Six and argued that she should play
some role in the establishment of a permanent fisheries marketing
policy.[3] Until mid-1970 the Community was so involved in finalizing
and working out the details of the Common Agricultural Policy that the
important fisheries sector had been allowed to operate more or less as it
had in the past. With the admission of Norway the Community becomes an exporter of fish.

FUTURE APPLICANTS

At the same time negotiations were under way to grant Britain,
Denmark, Ireland, and Norway formal associate membership, six other
members of EFTA were angling for a special relationship which would
give them status in the economic affairs of the Community without requiring economic and political integration. The most serious applicants
are Austria, Switzerland, and Sweden; Finland, Iceland, and Portugal are
seeking preferential treatment of some kind. Spain has recently sought
some special trade position with EC.

A precedent for special economic arrangements was set with Yugoslavia. Among other things, an agreement offered special treatment of
Yugoslav beef and veal products on a quota basis and permitted other
products to move on an open basis in accordance with tariff rates set
under the General Agreement on Tariffs and Trade (GATT).

AUSTRIA

The European Community takes 41 percent of Austria's exports and
supplies 56 percent of her imports. Austria therefore seeks a far-reaching
economic arrangement with the Community but because of her treaty
obligations does not want to become involved in the political aspects of
the Community. She also intends to retain her lucrative trading arrangements with Eastern Europe, especially Hungary and Bulgaria.

SWITZERLAND

Switzerland is in much the same position, guarding her political
neutrality most vigorously and shying away from anything resembling

---

3. The accession agreement provides for a reopening and a review of the Community fisheries policy with Norway participating in the new arrangement. On Sep-
tember 25, 1972, Norway voters in a referendum on the Common Market rejected
membership by 53.4 to 46.6 percent. Though the referendum is not binding on Parliament which makes the final decision, observers suggest that Parliament will follow

an obligation to follow the Community in foreign policy. At present 45 percent of Switzerland's total trade is with the European Community; with its enlargement her stake will be more than 60 percent. The Swiss make no secret of wanting all the economic advantages in the Community they can get while avoiding institutional involvements. An arrangement with Nigeria which skirts the institutional issues but provides far-reaching economic arrangements offers the Swiss a precedent.[4]

SWEDEN

Sweden is yet another case. With industry dominating the economic outlook, some of her leaders argue that Sweden, whether neutral or not, cannot long avoid moving into full associate membership. There is some indication that Sweden, with British entry formally assured, will seek full membership and attempt through negotiation with the enlarged Community to define the limitations imposed by her neutrality. About 40 percent of Sweden's foreign trade is with EFTA and 30 percent with the Market countries. With the admission of Britain and the other applicants, EFTA will disappear and Sweden, an advanced industrial country, will be on the outside looking into the Community. Sweden would ask no special arrangements beyond those granted other applicants. At this point she apparently has settled for an industrial free trade area, leaving ticklish problems of an economic union for later.

FINLAND AND ICELAND

Finland, presently a member of EFTA, has Russia as a suspicious neighbor and must talk softly in Brussels. However, for the present Finland is insisting on equal rights with the other applicants who seek something less than associate membership but something more than special treatment for a limited number of products. Icelanders want nothing to do with the presently developing fisheries policy of the European Community but want free access for their own fish exports.

PORTUGAL

Portugal has asked for outright association with the Community. An active and important member of EFTA and an important agricultural producer and exporter with African colonial interests involved, Portugal is more of a special case than any of the others. The issues are largely political and concern colonial policy. The Portuguese argue that the colonial policy issue can only be raised at a later stage. However, at this point it does not appear likely that the Portuguese request for association will receive serious attention until the larger issues of the original applicants are cleared. Many of the issues involved in the rela-

---

election results and perhaps opt for associate membership and special arrangements similar to that of four other EFTA members.

4. See Chapter 11.

tions of the above-mentioned countries to the Common Market will be subjects of discussion by the enlarged Community.

The economic and political implications of these developments in Europe will be the subject of debate and speculation for years to come. Needless to say, the arrangements inherent in the European Community's decision to enlarge itself will create a market and an economic power beyond anything now existing in the world. Whether this power is expressed in political terms or remains only economic, it will profoundly affect the political patterns of the world. Sufficient here that we speculate on the implications of this from an agricultural standpoint with special reference to the United States.

EFFECTS ON U.S. AGRICULTURE

Any prediction as to the ultimate effect of the enlarged Community on agricultural imports is certainly hazardous. It does appear that the enlarged Community will be even more self-sufficient and perhaps more of an agricultural exporting area than the EC has been in the past. The Community now produces surpluses in most basic crops and is over-supplied on a seasonal basis with fresh fruits and vegetables. In a book published in 1962, Lawrence B. Krause of the Brookings Institution pointed out that the six countries of the Common Market prior to the Treaty of Rome increased their production by 65 percent between 1948 and 1958. The consumption of farm products grew by only 40 percent. This increase resulted from the domestic agricultural policies of each country. However, after the inauguration of the Common Agricultural Policy he predicted the import replacement in these same countries in 1963–64 would be in farm products valued at $340 million. He estimated the annual loss of farm sales to the United States in 1956–66 would be $150–200 million. It was an erroneous prediction. Agricultural exports from the United States to the Community reached their highest point in history in that year, due primarily to the increase in feed grain and soybean imports. The same author predicted a drop of $200 million annually in grain imports from the United States. This has proven correct, but due to the aforementioned increase in oilseeds, tobacco, and feed grains, the total agricultural imports by the Community have held at around $1–1.5 billion over the twelve-year period and reached an unprecedented $1.77 billion in fiscal year 1970.

On the basis of previous trade patterns the admission of Great Britain should mean an even larger import volume into the Community, especially of bread grains. This assumption, however, may be in error if the Community buys hard wheat for blending purposes and sells its soft wheat in third-country markets or uses it for feed grain. Subsidies are now being provided in the Community for denaturing soft wheat and using it for feed grain. If continued on a large scale this will eventually reduce the demand for feed grains from the United States and other exporting countries.

The Economic Research Service of the USDA has projected the British farm production pattern to 1975 on its present arrangements compared to estimated production under EC membership. A base of 1959–63 was set up, and the average annual cereal production for that period was 9.5 million tons. Under present policies this figure would grow to 15.2 million tons by 1975, and with EC membership the figure would approach 16.3 million tons. In the case of beef cattle the figure of 864,000 tons would rise to 1 million tons under present policies but drop to 963,000 tons under the EC. Mutton and lamb on the same basis would drop from 300,000 to 273,000 tons. Pork, poultry, meat, eggs, potatoes, and horticultural products would vary little, as would sugar and fresh milk production.[5]

In a later summary the Economic Research Service set out the dollar volume on the kinds of products U.S. agriculture supplied the British market. Great Britain, as the fifth largest dollar market for U.S. farm products, bought $454 million worth of products for the 1966–67 trade year. This figure exceeds that of imports from Great Britain to the United States by $425 million. The major U.S. exports were un-manufactured tobacco, $151 million; feed grains, $92 million; wheat and flour, $41 million; fruits and preparations, $25 million; and vegetables and preparations, $22 million. In the projection of total food imports by the EC membership, the Economic Research Service sees overall import requirements reduced significantly from what would be imported in 1975 if present policies were continued. Increases are seen, however, for lamb, bacon, canned ham, vegetable oils, fats and oils (excluding butter and lard), oilseeds, dried fruit, tomatoes, potatoes, and fresh and frozen vegetables. Market declines are indicated for beef, milk and milk products, lard, sugar, wheat (cut almost to one-half the present), feed grains, and citrus and other fruit.[6]

Some authorities believe the Community will adopt a less protective agricultural policy with Great Britain and her three partners admitted. They argue that increasing urbanization and higher food prices will force the larger Community to pay more attention to the consumer and less to the farm sector. It must be remembered, however, that each of the four applicants to the Community accepted without reservation the policies and institutions at the time of their applications. Since the Treaty of Rome is irrevocable and since the Community still operates by unanimous vote, it will take a major upheaval in present operations to change the situation.

The Agricultural Committee of the National Planning Association, in a review in 1963 of the probable effects of the Common Agricultural Policy, saw no immediate change in the Community trade policy: "With or without the British membership, current prospects are that the Common Market trade policy will be dictated by domestic agricultural policies. . . . Such policies, under the mandate of the Treaty of Rome,

5. Foreign and Foreign Regional Analysis Division, ERS, May 1968.
6. See ERS Bulletin 248, 1968.

most attempt to improve farm incomes relative to nonfarm incomes."
The paper concluded with the assertion that all present exporters will
face a more restrictive agricultural trade policy than now exists.[7]

7. *The European Common Market and American Agriculture*, Vol. II, No. 6.
National Planning Association, Sept. 1963.

Chapter 17

THE SHAPE OF THINGS TO COME

IN 1972, the last year before the formal enlargement of the Common Market, the original Six will have operated for twelve years under the Common Agricultural Policy (CAP) and fourteen years under the original first step at economic integration under the Rome Treaty. These years of actual common action on Community problems have seen little change in the original CAP promulgated in 1960. The same has been true on the industrial side, although industrial integration has moved more slowly. Expectation is small that the addition of the new members in 1973 will materially change the policies and procedures under which the Six have operated.

The new Community of Ten will have a population of nearly 300 million and a gross national product second only to the United States. It will have the largest volume of international trade of any area in the world—more than $50 billion exports and $49 billion imports. The combined output of motor vehicles and steel in the Ten will exceed that of any other area in the world. However, the Community will lag in such items as energy production, computer use, telephones per capita, and household appliances.

Some of the key issues which faced the Council of Ministers meeting in February 1970 when they hammered out their position for the beginning of the British negotiations following the Hague meeting in 1969 were still evident in late 1971 and early 1972. Some resolution of these issues was implied in the final negotiations with the British on admission, but there are still mountains to climb.

1. The kind of political integration or unity that will emerge in the enlarged Community.

2. Monetary reform and the extent of budget control the Commission at Brussels is to exercise over the national budget.

3. How to accelerate the objectives of a balanced income between urban and rural populations and how to handle the problem of agricultural surplus.

The French and German monetary problems in 1969, followed by the floating of the German Deutsche Mark in 1970 and mounting pressure on the American dollar in European money markets, brought the whole world monetary system to a near crisis. Inflation in the United States, the serious deficit in U.S. trade balance, and the continuing raid on the dollar by international speculators forced the United States into a new economic policy in 1971. The gold backing of the dollar was removed, and a surcharge of 10 percent was levied on all imports into the American market. This sudden and unheralded action by one of the strongest nations in the world threw the entire world in turmoil for a period of time. It shocked the Common Market members and most of the European partners of the United States in the loosely structured North Atlantic Treaty Organization (NATO). Fears swept Europe that the surcharge especially would result in a drastic drop of exports to the United States and would set off another world recession. Most of the European countries (Great Britain excepted) were experiencing a slowdown in the rather rapid economic growth of previous years. However, after some of the shock wore off and after many meetings, a sort of international compromise on currency revaluation by the ten major trading countries was arrived at late in December 1971. President Nixon, in a rather dramatic and unexpected announcement from Bermuda just prior to his conference with Prime Minister Heath of Great Britain, removed the surcharge (see Chapter 18 for details).

POLITICAL INTEGRATION

The question of political unity—when and how much—is always uppermost in the minds of those European countries that would like to have the economic advantages which the enlarged Market promises. This also concerns the United States and other great powers. Commission President Malfatti took note of this in a statement early in 1971:

We are often told that the Community is an economic giant without political responsibility. This criticism is only partly justified. Unification is still a long way off and we are inclined to conduct our relations with the rest of the world in the light of immediate and pressing needs only. The time is near when this shortcoming will have to be made good by a clear and institutionally defined political will.

After an agreement in 1965 to reorganize the Common Market institutions at Brussels, the Council of Ministers in late 1969 cut the Commission membership from fourteen to nine and renamed the executive body the European Commission. This change in the executive structure implied to some members that all negotiations with outside countries would be carried on by one spokesman whose position would be spelled out in advance. As the Council began to work under French chairmanship, serious differences were in evidence on the issue of governing the enlarged Community. Germany, on the one hand, insisted on a federal union similar in structure to the present Bonn government, with relatively centralized power at Brussels on those questions common to the whole area. This arrangement would permit some sort of monetary control or supervision and increase the power of the Parliament over the Community budget, social security system, and investment policies. France, on the other hand, was strongly committed to "a Europe of nation states" and insisted that the Commission at Brussels have power and jurisdiction over only those areas in the Community which the Council of Ministers have assigned to it by unanimous vote. France had a stalwart ally in Great Britain where budget and monetary reform were second only to the agricultural problem in the negotiations for membership. However, the idea of a truly federal union—at least something considerably more than an arrangement for political cooperation—is still attractive to the Germans, Italians, and Belgians. Outside the official French position there are individual moves which seek to modify the strict De Gaullist position of "a Europe of nation states."

Jean Monnet heads a committee for the United States of Europe composed mostly of older persons and those long devoted to greater European cooperation and broad contacts with the United States. The first aim of this committee is establishment of an American-European committee to discuss NATO problems, such as an international money system, the balance of payments, American investments in Europe, and an exchange of technology. Monnet's committee is presently considering another committee to build an institutional arrangement with the Soviet Union and provide for standing economic cooperation and expansion of trade and cultural relations with the Eastern European states. Paralleling these efforts to some extent, the Western European union seeks to develop a new road to European unity. Their final aim is development of an organization which stops short of federal union but is something much stronger than a confederation of states.

MONETARY REFORM

Budget and monetary reform is on the boards for step-by-step consideration in the enlarged Community. The form and extent of central fiscal control and a common monetary system will hinge on the form of unity that finally emerges in the enlarged Community. The problems of equalizing rural and urban incomes and living standards and of handling surplus agricultural products remain.

AGRICULTURAL PROTEST

The second Mansholt plan for structural change and equalizing urban and rural income was returned to the Commission for revision by the Council of Ministers in 1969. When the Commission met to review and revise the plan in March 1971, rumors spread throughout Europe that there would be no increase in farm prices and that the plan would "do away with little farmers." This brought some 80,000 irate farmers from all over Europe in protest against the anticipated action by the Commission. Though farmer protests against government policies are quite common in Europe (especially in France where dumping produce in the streets causing roadblocks is frequent), a gathering of 80,000 angered producers could not be ignored by the Council of Ministers.

All major decisions in agriculture—structural changes, prices, and market regulations—are made at the Community level by unanimous agreement of the Council of Ministers. No longer do individual nations determine their agricultural policy. But the need for unanimity makes decisions long in coming. Prices had not been raised in the Community for three years. Farmer anger at low prices plus fears for the future with the Mansholt plan triggered the march toward the one place protest might be effective—Common Market headquarters in Brussels. The protest was effective. Prices for milk were hiked 6 percent, grains 2–5 percent depending on the crop, and beef 10 percent in two stages extending over two years. The ministers also approved the Mansholt plan for structural change and authorized the first stage to begin immediately.

MANSHOLT PLAN

The core of the Mansholt proposal was to cut down the number of persons living on the land. Farmers over 55 years of age who gave up farming would be paid at least $1,000 per year; those under 55 who gave up farming would receive premiums of at least eight times the rental value of their land. Farm owners who took advantage of this proposal and leased their land for at least eighteen years to a holder receiving modernization would be entitled to a lump sum equal to 6 percent of nine years' rent. The land would be placed at the disposal of the European Community. It could be used for recreation or reforestation, or it could be made available to other farmers who wanted to enlarge and modernize their holdings. To encourage participation in the new program the Commission proposed a grant to each participant equal to 15 percent of the rent. The total cost of the program over the first five years was estimated at $2.1 billion. Tied into the overall program was a ban against extending the present agricultural acreage. Advice and training for new jobs would be given those leaving the farm. Grouping of small farms into producers' associations would be encouraged, but such cooperatives would not be exempt from the rules of competition set out in the Rome Treaty. Implementation of the proposal would be left to the member states. The preamble of the directives presented to the Council of Ministers for carrying out the program emphasized higher incomes and a better balance between industry and agriculture. It also hinted, but did not specifically say, that this would reduce surpluses. The same sort of change in farm size, modernization, and rapid application of new technology in the United States has consistently produced more surplus rather than less. It is too much to expect that a similiar move in Europe would do more, although it would, as in the United States, divide the total farm income among fewer people.

MODIFIED PLAN

The modified form of the plan as approved by the Council of Ministers in April 1971 sets a specific target: Each agricultural property throughout the six nations should be able at the end of a six-year period to provide as good an income for one or two full-time workers as is being received by industrial workers in the same region.

Four practical measures are provided in the initial stages of the plan.

1. Premiums will be paid per acre when good farmland is sold for attachment to a property in the process of being modernized. Premiums will also be paid for the removal of poor farmland from production.

2. $600 per year will be paid to any farmer or farm worker between the ages of 55 and 65 who abandons farming (other than personal gardening), 25 percent of this to be paid by the Community in regions regarded as economically normal. The bonus will go up to 65 percent in disaster regions as defined by the Community. Most of these regions are in Italy and France. However, the terms of the British accession to the Community provide special measures for hill farmers. In both France and West Germany discussions are under way to provide state subsidies rather than Community subsidies to the small producers. The balance of the indemnity for quitting farming is paid by the national governments.

3. Farmers presenting to the authorities a modernization plan likely to guarantee within six years or less revenue as good as the industrial workers in the same region may borrow needed capital at 3 percent interest. Such funds cannot be used for the purchase of land.

4. Each nation of the Six has pledged to maintain training programs and scholarships for all farmers in modern farming methods. The program calls for an expenditure of $285 million per year over a four-year period, at the end of which the program will be revised.

In the meantime, studies of the agricultural work force in the Community indicate that the number of people engaged in agriculture has decreased by one-third in the period 1960–69. Italy had a decrease of 38.5 percent, reflecting largely the decline of women and children working on farms. Italy still has 4 million farm workers and accounts for two-fifths of the work force on EC farms. France, with nearly one-half of the Community's land, accounts for 30 percent of the work force and experienced a decline of 28 percent in the 1960–69 period. West Germany declined 30 percent. One-third of this decline was in farm operators, 12 percent in hired workers, and 54 percent in family labor. Decrease in the farm labor force in the Netherlands was 27 percent, in Belgium 30 percent, and in Luxembourg 7 percent. Even with this rather dramatic reduction there are still 10.5 million farm workers in the Community.

AGRICULTURAL SURPLUS PROBLEM

Surpluses of butter, poultry, sugar, pork, and soft wheat at home and the subsidies required to dump them in third-country markets are eating away the upper limits of the $3 billion budget for supporting agriculture agreed on in December 1970. Most authorities agree that the higher protective policies involved in carrying out the social objectives spelled out by the Treaty of Rome are a major factor in the mounting surplus problem in the Community. Despite the problem of commodity surpluses, farm incomes have gone up and farms are slowly being modernized.

Butter is still the major problem. Farmers with small acreages under the system of intensive land use can keep a few cows and at Community dairy prices do fairly well financially. The cow, sow, and hen combination, now all but abandoned in American agriculture, is still the miracle maker for the small family unit in most of Europe. The cost of supporting butter prices and of exporting or storing the surplus reached close to $1 billion in 1969 and exceeded that figure in 1970. Rather drastic action was taken to increase consumption of butter in the summer of 1969 when an attempt was made to place a special tax on vegetable oils in hope of increasing the price of margarine and making butter more attractive from the price standpoint.

At present less drastic measures are being taken to reduce surpluses of butter and soft wheat. Bonuses are offered for the slaughter of dairy cows, and the Community herds have been cut by more than 200,000 head. This has not reduced the butter supply proportionately since European farmers usually slaughter their least productive animals, just as U.S. farmers put in the soil bank their less productive land and, by applying better methods, produce more. There has been an increased denaturing of soft wheat which now replaces to some extent feed grain imports from the United States and other exporting countries. The Commission in late 1970 published a Common Market balance sheet on the principal feed grains (see Table 17.1). It showed an increased denaturing of wheat to an estimated total of 4 million tons in 1971. It also projected imports of some 14.7 million tons of various grains and exports of 7.2 million tons of the same grains.

TABLE 17.1
COMMON MARKET BALANCE OF PRINCIPAL GRAINS, 1970–71
(million metric tons)

	Soft Wheat	Durum	Barley	Corn	Rye	Total
Production	26.2	3.1	14.1	12.4	3.3	59.1
Stocks 8/1/70	2.6	0.1	0.6	1.5	0.9	5.7
Imports	2.7	1.3	1.6	8.7	0.2	14.5
Total Supply	31.5	4.5	16.3	22.6	4.4	79.3
Direct consumption	21.7	4.2	15.2	18.5	3.5	63.1
Denaturing	4.0	...	...	...	0.3	4.3
Exports	3.6	0.1	0.4	2.7	0.4	7.2
Stocks 7/31/71	2.2	0.2	0.7	1.4	0.2	4.7
Total Utilization	31.5	4.5	16.3	22.6	4.4	79.3

The administrators of Community programs in Brussels have generally held that only two or three methods can adequately control the surplus problem, and none of them is very palatable to the farmer or the politician. One alternative is straightforward production control with quotas for each country and each farmer in the Community. A second possibility is outright subsidy to the small farmer paid by his home nation instead of the Guarantee and Guidance Fund. This would mean that France or West Germany, which have many small and rather vocal farmers in their southern areas, would pay each small farmer a direct subsidy to increase his income and allow the larger farmers in the north to continue to make high profits under the present high-price system.

A third alternative would be to fix the prices of the principal crops at the world market level and permit unrestrained competition with outside producers. This, say some economists, would be popular with outside exporting countries but would drive many smaller and some of the larger European farmers to the wall. It would also mean abandoning the Common Market's objective of raising the living standard of the rural population and equalizing the labor income of urban and rural populations. Most Common Market nations have always shied away from direct production or market controls except in the case of sugar which is controlled under an international agreement. It is improbable that direct production control would be politically possible at the present time.

The scheme of subsidizing the smaller farmers in return for some cut in production seems to be one way out. This is being considered somewhat independently in France. The scheme would tax the large sugar and grain producers in northern France and subsidize the smaller farmers in the south. A similar scheme is under discussion in West Germany. This is the probable compromise solution between the long-range Mansholt plan and outright production control. As for dropping the variable levy system and the present protection in the market (as many outsiders and exporting countries wish), it is as unlikely to happen as is U.S. agriculture to turn to an unrestricted world market.

Considering the built-in rigidities of the CAP, the absence of international agreement on nontariff barriers, and the coming enlargement of the Community, it may be helpful to speculate on the future for agriculture in the Community.

FUTURE FOR AGRICULTURE

The agricultural staff of the General Agreement on Tariffs and Trade (GATT), which keeps foreign developments under continuous review, is somewhat alarmed at the pattern and mechanics of foreign agricultural trade in the Community. The present system (as explained in Chapter 9) is something of a "special preference" arrangement which places trade with outside countries, specifically the Eastern European bloc, in rather rigid trade arrangements between the Community and a country with a special interest in some product. For instance, Germany may want to increase her industrial trade with Poland and make a special arrangement to receive Polish cattle under preferential treatment up to a certain volume. France wants to sell cars to Hungary and will take in return cattle, fresh fruits, or other products up to a certain amount. Or Greece seeking outlets for her processed orange and lemon juice will take agreed amounts of sunflower seed from Romania. All of these individual arrangements are cleared by the proper authorities and presently are negotiated by the Commission in Brussels. They are simple bilateral arrangements between the Community and a country and not multilateral arrangements except when the Eastern European country happens to be a member of GATT. "The danger is," say GATT officials, "that this system will continue, and far from moving toward a freer and easier exchange of goods between countries . . . foreign trade with the Community will continue to be a patchwork and crazy quilt of preference arrangements as the interests of each member in the Community dictates."

Individuals responsible for carrying out the CAP see the continuation of these arrangements along with the variable levy system and continued use of export subsidies on surplus agricultural products in third-country markets. They argue that there will be continuing pressure from farmers to increase grain prices since most other grains and the livestock, dairy, and poultry industries are intimately tied to the bread grain price. This could set off demands for increased prices and protection all along the line. Most observers believe that this pressure will be resisted and that the external tariff rates negotiated in the Kennedy Round will remain stable. It is unlikely that future negotiations will do much to reduce these barriers. Under present GATT rules the Community may change to levies under the same conditions as an individual state. This means not only that the Community may raise or lower the variable levy for reasons of its own protection but that outside countries which are damaged by such action have redress under the GATT rules. Nearly all the states which applied for membership in the Community in the early period sought entrance on their own terms or with only slight modification of their own system of agricultural income protection. This was especially true of Great Britain. Now even Great Britain is willing to accept membership on the basis of the present policy, with a minimum period for adjustment.

What are the implications for the United States and other major agricultural exporting countries? The answers require some speculation on probable population growth, increased efficiency in farming, trade policies of the enlarged Community, and the extent to which individual governments within the Community put resources into agricultural production.

Probably the best estimate of production and trade in the future is found in the studies of the Organization for Economic Cooperation and Development (OECD). The agricultural ministers of the OECD who met in Paris in November 1968 received a staff report projecting production and trade to 1975 and 1985. The secretariat staff had concluded that "on the basis of present policies, the agriculture in the OECD [the membership of which included the Common Market] is likely to expand its output faster than the population and increased food consumption growth in the area." This estimate was reaffirmed at meetings in 1969 and 1970.

Food production in excess of internal requirements, now about 20 million tons per year, represents 6 percent of gross production. By 1985 the increase will reach 120 million tons per year or 21 percent of production. In the case of butter, export availabilities in terms of butterfat (now about 150,000 tons) would rise to 375,000 tons in 1975. There would be about the same percentage rise in solid nonfat milk. It was felt that structural changes under way in the EC and other countries of OECD might slow down the milk production beyond 1975, with the net export availability dropping to 4–6 percent of total production. It was pointed out that these percentages were of marginal importance. Translated into tonnage they amount to a considerable export trade. Using the Food and Agriculture Organization of the United Nations projection for world food requirements in 1975, the top figure would not exceed 27 million tons or less than one-fourth of the net availability of food products in the OECD area. Only one exception was made to the rather dire predictions of oversupply—beef and veal products, which are in growing demand throughout the OECD area. The OECD ministers noted that "it is no longer possible for a member country to improve the incomes of its rural population by increasing production only but that other measures would have to be taken to control supply, such as direct government intervention, land retirement, the limitation of price guarantees, specified quantities per farm, or direct restrictions of quantities supplied per farm."

The section of the OECD report on restrictions of the movement of agricultural products in international trade was even more doleful. "In spite of some efforts at discipline made by common consent or unilaterally imposed, agricultural trade is carried out in a most unhealthy environment." The various import restrictions are being reinforced rather than relaxed. The report noted that "an alarming picture emerges of measures taken to facilitate exports. In some commodity sectors there is no single member country which does not sell—or has arrangements for selling—abroad below the prices ruling on the home market."

Since the United States is a founding member of the OECD, U.S. trade and production policies must bear the same measure of censure as those of other countries. If we are to endorse even a part of the views of the OECD study group, the conclusion must be that even greater trouble is ahead for American agriculture. Nothing short of a genuine worldwide coordinated attack on production and distribution problems can prevent disaster to producers in the developed areas from overproduction and in some of the developing countries from starvation. Nothing short of a genuine international effort can begin to rationalize agriculture.

It seems unlikely that the kind of cooperation politically possible in the larger Community will have any real effect on the agricultural problem. Whatever form the enlarged Community takes in terms of community financing, political integration, and reconciliation of social security and other national laws, the problem of managing the agricultural surplus will remain the center of concern.

So far as the practical effect of the enlargement of the Common Market on international trade is concerned, even the most friendly of the Six admit that the Common Market will discriminate to a certain extent against the United States. The most critical area is farm exports which account for about one-fourth of all U.S. sales abroad. United States agricultural trade with the enlarged Community will be squeezed, although British membership (the largest food importer in the world) will dilute by about 5 percent the present self-sufficiency of the area. In the lineup taking form, sugar producers of Sweden, Austria, Switzerland, Portugal, and New Zealand will enjoy benefits denied the United States and Canada. In addition to the increased production of wheat and other grains within the Market area, the heavily subsidized exports of grains, pork, poultry, and dairy products in third markets forces heavier subsidies by the United States to meet competition. American citrus sales to the EC have dropped because of preferences given to Spain, Tunisia, Morocco, and Israel. Pressure will increase here as producers in some of the British possessions in the Caribbean and Africa press for preferences. Other American products such as tobacco run into tariffs erected to protect French and Italian producers. In the many talks of EC leaders and officials with U.S. interests, little or no encouragement was noted that the CAP will change.

The dramatic visits of President Nixon to Peking and Moscow in early 1972 with the subsequent moves to open up trade between the United States and the Communist nations will reduce the pressure for more open agricultural trade between the United States and the European Community, since it is evident that some of our surplus grains will go to Russia and China. However, the basic issue—that of a low fixed tariff vs the flexible levy system—will continue to be the main flash point between the two trading areas.

Chapter 18

NEW TRADE LEGISLATION

⚔

LEGISLATION to replace the expired Trade Expansion Act of 1962 has traveled a rocky and troublesome road. Protectionist feeling in the United States has been rising sharply, partly because liberalization of trade has affected some industries and labor groups adversely. Rising prices, unemployment, deficit international trade balances, and general business slowdown during the early 1970s have added to the pressures for more protection. Legislation proposed by President Johnson in 1968 and by President Nixon in 1969 carried provisions to assist U.S. industries adversely affected by our liberal trade policy.

The major revisions undertaken by the Johnson administration in 1968 were in behalf of more flexibility and greater power for the President in implementing the escape clause, aiding domestic businesses which were seriously affected by previous tariff reductions, and eliminating the American selling price procedure for establishing tariff rates. Other devices enlarged the powers, originally given in 1962, that permitted the President to give or take away tariff privileges from any nation whose practices seriously damaged domestic concerns. There was also provision for some liberalization of trade with Eastern European countries and the Soviet Union.

Hearings were held by both houses of Congress during 1968. In those hearings protectionist sentiment mounted, based on fears that the reductions in the Kennedy Round would impair domestic industry. With the largely unworkable provisions for relief to injured industries in the 1962 act, it became evident that any measure passing the 1968 Congress would be loaded with amendments and restrictions to protect

152

special segments of the economy. Many bills and amendments sought relief for specific agricultural products, drugs, cement, paper, aluminum, steel, oil, and chemicals. The rush to get home to the general elections in the fall of 1968 and the crowded congressional calendar had much to do with the failure of the bill to reach the floor of the Congress. It appears, however, that a tacit agreement developed between the executive office and congressional leaders to the effect that if the trade bill were not brought up, the many special bills calling for added protection for U.S. industries and agriculture would not be pressed. To all intents and purposes, the matter was left to the new administration coming to power in January 1969.

NIXON ADMINISTRATION

President Nixon, pressed with many domestic issues, the Vietnam war, turmoil in the colleges and universities, and unrest in the cities, did not initiate any new moves in trade policy early in his administration. No special task force was set up to look into the matter. A quiet review of the existing situation was made by the executive departments most concerned. Trade policy was definitely in a low priority. This was quite a contrast to the new administration in 1961 when a task force had, prior to inauguration, developed a far-reaching international trade policy based on the Grand Design of Atlantic Unity and a politically unified Europe (see Chapter 7). It was not until November 1969 that the Nixon administration made its move on international trade. The flurry of bills introduced in 1968 and 1969 which sought to protect U.S. industry and agriculture, others which proposed freer trade with Eastern Europe, and the extension of the presidential power under the old Trade Expansion Act of 1962 were frowned upon. The President, in his message to Congress November 18, noted that the United States had steadily pursued freer trade for the past thirty-five years, and after a "review of that policy the administration finds its continuation to be in our national interest. At the same time, it is clear that trade problems of the 1970s will differ from those in the past. New developments in the rapidly evolving world economy will require new responses and new initiatives."

In support of this contention, the President cited three main factors:

1. World economic interdependence has become a fact. Reduction in tariffs and transportation costs have internationalized the world economy to a high degree.

2. A number of foreign countries now compete fully with the United States in world markets.

3. The traditional surplus in U.S. balance of trade has disappeared.

Nixon rejected the argument that we should abandon our traditional approach to freer trade, not only because he "believed in the principle of freer trade, but for the very pragmatic reason that any reduction of imports to the United States brought about by restrictions not accepted by our trading partners would bring reaction against our exports—all quite legally."

The measure which went before the Congress as the Trade Act of 1970 was much different from the President's original draft. The President had made four specific recommendations which gave the executive office greater power. He asked for (1) restoration of the authority of the Chief Executive to make limited tariff reductions, such authority having expired with the Trade Expansion Act of 1962 on June 30, 1967; (2) authority to take immediate and concrete steps to reduce nontariff barriers to trade; (3) power to make more workable the original provisions in our trade acts to assist domestic industries unduly affected by lower tariffs on imports; (4) the U.S. portion of GATT costs to be funded by direct budget appropriation rather than through contingency funds of the President.

The arguments in the President's message in suppport of these changes pointed out that in the first instance he was not calling for authority to reduce tariffs on a major scale. Present conditions, he said, demanded that he have authority to make minor adjustments in individual situations from time to time. As an illustration, he cited the necessity to raise the duty on an article as a result of an escape clause action or when statutory changes are made in tariff classifications. Such authority had expired with the Trade Expansion Act.

As a first assault on nontariff barriers the President asked for elimination of the American selling price system of customs valuation on a few American products—mainly benzoid chemicals. The elimination of this system, the President said (and his argument is supported by GATT negotiators, veterans of the Kennedy Round), would bring reciprocal reductions in foreign tariffs on U.S. chemical exports. It would also mean a reduction in important European nontariff barriers, such as road taxes, as well as elimination of the preferential treatment on tobacco accorded by the United Kingdom to the countries of the Commonwealth.[1]

While it was not spelled out in the act, Nixon's proposal implied that the President would have power to act on the whole subject of nontariff barriers. There is some dispute as to whether the authority to negotiate tariff rates spelled out in previous acts also included the right to negotiate on nontariff issues (see Chapter 14). Some countries insist

---

1. Certain tariff reductions in the Kennedy Round do not become effective until the U.S. selling price system is abolished. Reduction in tobacco tariffs in Great Britain is an example. Due to the controversy over the Trade Act of 1970 the United States has not taken action on this. The Council of Ministers of the Six recently gave the United States one more year to try to make some headway in removing this provision of our customs taxes.

that nontariff devices serve purely national purposes and are not subject to international regulations. The U.S. Congress always has retained control over quotas and other devices used to protect a particular industry, and Congress has been reluctant to give the executive office much leeway in dealing with this problem. If the American selling price system of valuation is eliminated, this presumably will open the way for the executive office to undertake negotiations in GATT at some time in the future to deal with nontariff barriers. The President's message specifically called upon the legislative branch for a general declaration of legislative intent on nontariff barriers to assist in efforts to obtain lowering of such barriers. It was pointed out that this declaration of intent was not to bypass Congress but to strengthen the U.S. negotiating position. Congress would be kept informed in any such negotiations, and any agreements that required new legislation would be submitted to the Congress.

The administration approached the hearings before the Ways and Means Committee by giving the interested officials in the executive branch an opportunity to argue their points of view. Maurice Stans, Secretary of Commerce, advocated quotas for textile imports, a position consistent with the Nixon campaign promise to "do something about textiles." Stans also recognized a need for some protection for the shoe industry. Interior Department witnesses hinted at the continued need for quotas on oil imports; Clifford Hardin, Secretary of Agriculture, spoke strongly for continued open trade arrangements. Secretary of State William Rogers and Carl J. Gilbert, the President's Special Representative in Trade Negotiations, preferred the original Nixon proposal of 1969 which gave the President more power and flexibility in solving trade problems, but they shied away from congressionally imposed quotas. These hearings repeated once more the process which has become a tradition in U.S. trade legislation—namely that U.S. trade policy usually results from a compromise between special interests both outside and inside the government and is markedly short term. In early 1971 Nixon established a Council of International Economic Policy. It is hoped that this Council of business leaders and international traders may bring U.S. foreign trade policy into better focus.

ADVANTAGES

The Trade Expansion Act of 1962 attempted to provide relief to industries adversely affected by foreign imports on two counts: the escape clause provisions, and the adjustment assistance. Neither of the provisions has worked to the satisfaction of those adversely affected. The escape clause provisions have been so rigidly interpreted that the U.S. Tariff Commission has not recommended a single case for relief. The adjustment assistance provisions of the 1962 act provide for loans, technical assistance, tax relief, allowances for relocation, training, and

direct aid to injured industries. Little has actually happened, because of
the difficulty of getting a final judgment on injury and the necessity for
relief through the bureaucracy. In the new law the "substantial cause"
criterion would be less stringent than the "primary cause" provision
under the 1967 act. The Tariff Commission would continue to gather
statistics and factual information. The determination of whether
assistance is given or withheld would be made by the President. Existing adjustment provisions would be extended to units of multiplant
companies and workers.

Section 252 of the 1962 Trade Expansion Act authorizes the
President to impose duties or other import restrictions on products of
any nation which places unjustified restrictions on U.S. agricultural
products. Such authority was used during the Johnson administration
in the so-called chicken war. After a finding by the Tariff Commission,
the United States raised duties on Volkswagen trucks from Germany
and certain wines and other products from France in order to obtain
compensation for damages to the poultry industry. The new act would
extend the authority to all U.S. products. This would be a major tool
for the President in dealing, for example, with the textile problem posed
by Japan's exports. Since Japanese imports to the United States sub-
stantially affect the U.S. textile industry, he would have the power to
"take appropriate action" against Japan or any nation which subsidizes
competition in third-country markets when such competition unfairly
affects U.S. exports.

The provision for formal and specific appropriations in GATT
rather than continued reliance on contingency financing serves two
purposes: it arms the United States with powerful devices for retaliation and a major trade war if the EC or other nations move in that
direction; at the same time, it moves toward greater permanency, and
perhaps greater use, of the GATT and multilateral negotiations to
stabilize world trade and make it "freer."

INTERIM POLICY

Rising protectionist pressure largely from agriculture, shoe manufacturers, and textile interests using artificial fiber has forced the Nixon
administration to an interim policy which, in effect, has divergent trade
goals. The interim policy affects all countries to which the United
States exports goods and from which imports are received. The principal focus, however, is on the European Community and Japan. Both
have made serious inroads into the markets of the U.S. textile industry.
The EC, with its flexible levy system and value-added tax system, can
prevent expansion of U.S. agricultural trade and in fact is likely to
force a substantial decline in agricultural exports to that area. Stans
early in 1969 undertook a personal tour of the EC in an effort to achieve

a voluntary resolution of these troublesome problems. He urged elimination or reduction of nontariff barriers and argued for increased trade between the United States and the Community. His specific idea was to initiate talks looking to voluntary restraint on exports of artificial fiber textiles to the United States. The idea of such a voluntary agreement was cooly received by European governments, and individual textile enterprises were even less receptive. In West Germany textile producers pointed out that they were no better off in regard to imports from outside their country than the United States. West Germany in 1968 imported textiles worth $24 for each German citizen, compared to imports of $7 per citizen in the United States. Stans found even less enthusiasm for a voluntary agreement on agricultural products. The reason he wanted the agreement was obvious. For U.S. agricultural products to sell in EC countries necessitates heavy subsidies plus payment of high levies. The EC's flexible levy and value-added tax systems hold prices of farm products well above world market levels. From the EC view, any voluntary agreement would be at its expense. After two years of haggling, the United States and Japan in December 1971 reached an agreement to restrict imports of Japanese textiles in the United States, thus nullifying one of the main issues in the Trade Bill of 1970.

As was pointed out in an earlier chapter, U.S. agricultural exports to the EC showed a steady climb during the first four years of the transition period and have held at levels in excess of $1.3 billion since. This represents the largest single hard-currency market for U.S. agricultural exports, exceeded only by the combined exports to Canada, Japan, and the United Kingdom.

It is indeed difficult, depending upon where one sits, to determine what is "fair and reasonable" when a particular segment of a country's industry or agriculture is affected. What seems "fair and reasonable" in the overall view does not so appear to the individual concerned. The problems of agricultural exports to the EC are of deep concern, especially with the admission of Great Britain and three other high-producing agricultural countries to the Community. This was reflected in the addresses many of the U.S. government personnel made before agricultural groups in 1969 and 1970. Nathaniel Samuels, Deputy Under Secretary of State for Economic Affairs, said, "Agriculture is in search of a diplomacy. This must be a diplomacy to which a structure of production and exchange will be relevant to the interdependence of contemporary life, not only geographic in terms of communication but in the interacting patterns of investment production and trade." Thus Samuels opened up publicly the issue which concerns European and many other countries, including the developing nations—namely, that the free movement of capital investment is just as essential in the modern world as is the freer movement of goods in trade. European countries have viewed the rush of American capital to get behind the protective wall of the EC with some alarm.

When the House Ways and Means Committee version of the 1970 Trade Act passed the House in late 1970, mild diplomatic language gave way to alarm and open threats of a trade war between the European Community and the United States. Peter Tennant, director general of the British Export Council, in a speech before the American Chamber of Commerce in London on November 19, 1970, said: "I see retaliation happening willy-nilly in a massive way. The bill invites retaliation the moment it has Presidential assent and retaliation in a form which many congressmen and many Americans will regret. It has the seed in it for a bitter trade war." It is not a minor matter, Tennant argued, "when the textile and shoe provisions of the measure alone would affect $550 million shoe and textile exports of the European Community and in the worst hypothesis at least $1.9 million in Community trade in automobiles would be threatened."

Europeans were not the only ones expressing alarm at the possible consequences of the trade bill as passed. Some 4,000 members of the American Economic Association signed a letter to President Nixon protesting the enactment of restrictive legislation. In the economists' view the proposed legislation would invite retaliation and damage the American economy more than it would help any segment of it. Farmers in the Middle West with an important market for soybeans, cotton, and feed grains at stake in the Common Market and Japan were also openly opposed to the measure. At the same time they protested the protectionist stance of the Common Market on agricultural products. The major farm groups (American Farm Bureau, National Grange, National Farmer's Union, National Farmers Organization) and several commodity groups have criticized the measure. The most controversial provision of the House Ways and Means Committee bill which carried most of the provisions in the original Nixon proposal had to do with almost mandatory action by the President to impose quotas and higher tariffs on shoes and textile imports. Under the score of amendments which were attached to the measure, this same provision would apply to seventy other industrial items in the United States.

REACTION OF EUROPEAN COMMUNITY

The hard posture the United States has assumed, backed by potentially powerful arms for retaliation, is not taken lightly by EC leaders. Statements and a formal paper from the EC were delivered to U.S. Ambassador Robert J. Schaetzel in February 1970, reviewing relations between the United States and the Community: "Economic and commercial relations between the United States and the Community are causing concern on both sides of the Atlantic."

The paper was designed to correct "fairly profound misconceptions" about the effect of European integration on economic factors in the United States; it contained statistics showing that U.S. trade had fared better with the Community and had shown greater and more consistent growth than American trade with any other part of the world.

Total U.S. trade with the Community amounted to $13 billion in 1969—three times the total trade between the United States and the same six countries in 1958. From 1958 to 1969 U.S. exports to the Community grew by 182 percent, with a favorable balance of payments average for the period of $1.2 billion; U.S. exports to EFTA countries increased by 143 percent, and free trade with the rest of the world by only 118 percent.

The EC paper noted that the rising standard of living, which went hand in hand with an enlarged Market, was a major factor in the great increases of U.S. trade with the Community. Other factors were the Community's low common tariffs and the trade policy which resulted from major tariff negotiations. Indeed, the Community has ended up with the lowest tariffs among the industrialized nations of the world. The Commission paper also emphasized the leading role the Community has played in granting tariff preferences to developing nations and called upon all industrialized nations to take similar action.

However, the Commission paper was less positive in dealing with the agricultural sector. Statistics were marshaled to show that the hurt claimed by the United States was more imagined than actual. In 1968, as an example, the Community imported $1.4 billion worth of U.S. agricultural products; although there was a drop in 1967 from the high point of $1.6 million imported in 1966, American agricultural exports worldwide were lower. The U.S. share of total agricultural imports in the Community remains steady: 22 percent in 1964, 23 percent in 1966, and 22 percent in 1968, with 40 percent of U.S. exports entering the Community duty free. The heavy subsidies the Community and the United States pay to meet competition in third-country markets received little attention, although the paper noted that "at the present, agricultural market for agricultural products is more the scene of rivalry between public treasuries than competition between producers."

Something of an answer to the Community's paper of February 1970 was given by Gilbert before the 26th session of the Contracting Parties for GATT in Geneva in early 1970 in the course of an extended review of agricultural problems related to GATT:

> My government considers that agricultural trade must now come to the forefront in the work of contracting parties. It is precisely in this area that we may find the greatest scope for strengthened observance of GATT commitments and possibly new approaches to the coordination of agricultural policies as they affect trade. A degree of success in coping with agricultural problems may well be essential to the future viability of GATT.
>
> We must find a way to curb the use of extravagant subsidies. Their growing use in some areas had already led to serious distortions of world trade. My country has the choice of expanding the use of this same device or of convincing other areas (principally the EC) that they should curb the practice.

The Contracting Parties of GATT have authority to meet, discuss, and review the work of the various committees on agricultural and other sectors. They do not have the authority to negotiate settlements. The authority to negotiate, in the case of the United States, comes from Congress and the President; in the case of most other countries, from the government after a general agenda is agreed upon as to what the negotiations will be about. In the meantime, the American government and interested citizens and organizations are exploring alternate courses in U.S. policy—courses which could increase world trade and at the same time afford some measure of protection for certain domestic industries, especially agriculture.

Not as much has been said publicly about the increasing number of preferences granted by EC to particular countries on specific products outside the GATT rules. Preferences were granted by members or the Community on a bilateral basis during the transition period, but now such trade arrangements are negotiated by the Community as a unit. The Council, meeting in February 1970, implemented the policy spelled out in Article 113 of the Treaty of Rome which provided that at the end of the transition period, the EC should set up a commercial trade policy and that negotiations of the commercial agreements should be undertaken by the Commission in consultation with a special committee appointed by the Council. The Council on the same date adopted a trade agreement with Yugoslavia which gave special treatment to Yugoslavian meat of "baby beef" quality, with the understanding that Yugoslavia would respect certain requirements concerning quality, price, and rate of delivery. During the same three-day session, France was authorized to undertake certain negotiations in behalf of the Community with Japan.

It therefore appears evident that as the United States enters the decisive year of 1973 on trade legislation, the divisive and troublesome domestic issues are going to be paralleled by equally difficult and troublesome relationships with the Common Market. This is bound to materially affect our future trade policy.[2]

---

2. While the so-called Mills Bill, a version of President Nixon's suggested Trade Bill of 1969, passed the House, it failed to reach the hearing stage in the Senate in 1970. See next chapter for status of all trade legislation.

Chapter 19

Future U.S. Trade Policy

THE SINGLE-MINDED PURSUIT of open and freer international trade which
for thirty-eight years had characterized U.S. trade policy, no matter
what the administration in power, came to an abrupt halt temporarily
on August 15, 1971, when President Richard M. Nixon announced a
new economic policy for the United States. At the core of his international trade position were removal of the gold backing of the U.S. dollar (allowing the dollar to float in the international money market) and
imposition of a 10 percent surcharge on all imports to the United States.
This drastic action was prompted by an estimated $2 billion deficit in
the U.S. balance of payments with other nations (the largest in U.S.
history); a continuing drain on U.S. gold reserves brought on by speculators; and the fears of international bankers (especially in Europe) that
rising labor costs, inflation, and overcommitment of the United States
would sooner or later force devaluation of the dollar. This unheralded
step brought violent and sharp reaction from many of the principal U.S.
trading partners in the free world as well as concern by leading economists and some groups in the United States. Leading senators from the
farm states, both Democrat and Republican, feared retaliation from the
Common Market and Japan against U.S. agricultural exports; other
supporters of a liberal international trade policy feared encouragement
of the growing protectionism and isolation in the United States. Some
prominent U.S. economists were particularly opposed to the surcharge.
Paul Samuelson of Massachusetts Institute of Technology said, "It is a
bad way to negotiate." Paul Wallich of Yale University said, "The surcharge is counter-productive." Milton Friedman of University of Chi-

son? said, "It should never have been put on in the first place." Referring to Secretary of the Treasury John B. Connally's statement as to what would be required to lift the surcharge, Samuelson observed, "What depresses me is that we do not have the power behind the weight we are swinging around."

The administration's first price for removing the surcharge, as stated by then Treasury Secretary Connally, was indeed a high one. The demand, almost an ultimatum, was that:

1. Our principal trading partners, especially Germany and Japan, would have to revalue their currencies upward by about 12 percent so that American goods could enter world markets on a more competitive basis. Thus imports of foreign goods into the United States would be more costly and therefore would be reduced.

2. Our trading partners, especially the European nations, should bear a greater portion of the cost of their own defense.

3. Trade barriers—taxes, levies, quotas, and other impediments—against U.S. goods should be eliminated, especially on agricultural products.

This was to be accomplished without formal devaluation of the dollar, and the surcharge would not be removed until the trade deficit had been reversed.

REACTION TO NEW U.S. POLICY

The announcement provoked hurried and somewhat harried meetings and hastily prepared public statements by statesmen throughout most of the trading world (especially in Japan and the Common Market) as various groups began considering countermeasures. Stock exchanges in Japan, London, Paris, and Frankfurt were closed on the announcement. Within weeks factories in Germany, Canada, and Japan which depended largely on exports to the United States began closing down or laying off workers. The American dollar dropped by about 9 percent after the exchanges opened, and the value of the Japanese yen and the German mark rose sharply.

There was considerable talk about this setting off a major recession in Europe which was already experiencing some slowdown of industrial growth. However, most of the dire predictions did not actually come about, and a flurry of diplomatic activity on the part of the Common Market partners and some hasty bargaining by the United States blunted some of the harsher impact of this unorthodox move by the largest trading nation in the world. The U.S. Treasury fanned out special envoys to explain the new economic policy to our partners in Europe and Asia. The Common Market countries, including the new prospective members, held meetings to develop a common front on the monetary policy with a demand for removal of the 10 percent surcharge. Unable to agree in detail on the kind of monetary reform the new Community of Ten would eventually support, the foreign ministers were unanimous in demanding removal of the surcharge. Representative Wilbur D. Mills, chairman of the powerful House Ways and Means Committee, warned Secretary Connally to settle the trade issue fast. "To let the situation bog down would run the risk of an historic reversal of the move toward freer trade on the part of the United States." That movement, he pointed out, has helped underwrite an expansion of world trade from $55 billion twenty years ago to $300 billion today.

Representatives of banking and industrial enterprises attending the National Foreign Trade Convention in New York during the crisis in late October generally supported the administration's move, especially the initiative to obtain a realignment of currencies. There was wide support for Secretary Connally's hard-line stance that the import surcharge would remain until new exchange rates more favorable to the United States were agreed upon and certain unspecified nontariff barriers to U.S. goods were removed.

However, at the meeting of the Common Market's ten finance ministers in Rome in early November, Connally had somewhat softened his stand on dollar devaluation and suggested a hypothetical devaluation of the American dollar of about 9 percent.[1] This indicated to the Common Market and Japan that perhaps the United States would devaluate upon some common agreement to allow a general realignment of exchange rates. The November meeting between President Nixon and French President Georges Pompidou in the Azores removed the word *hypothetical* in their communique at the close of their talks, suggesting that the United States was ready to trade on the dollar devaluation. Pompidou withdrew his objection to beginning trade talks immediately, something he had blocked at the Brussels meeting of the Ten one week before. The United States had been pressing for immediate talks on trade problems, especially agricultural trade.

The Common Market countries, especially France, had been insisting that the Common Market nations were too busy with the admission of new members to "engage in another Kennedy Round of major trade negotiations until the mid-1970s." In the meantime, U.S. representatives on the Trade Committee of the Organization for Economic Cooperation and Development (OECD) were insisting that an agenda for examination of long-term trade questions be drawn up by that body.[2]

---

1. Only the United States Congress can change the gold backing of the American dollar; in final analysis any agreement on a figure is subject to congressional action. Congress passed the devaluation law in March 1972; President Nixon signed it March 22.

2. Secretary of State Rogers proposed in summer of 1971, and the OECD agreed to establish, the Trade Committee to review and survey long-term trade problems. Its first meeting was being held during the Nixon-Pompidou talks in the Azores.

Pompidou agreed to this. However, there seemed to be little softening of the Common Market line, again insisted upon by France, that the Common Agricultural Policy (CAP) would be modified in any major way in any of the immediate or long-term negotiations.

In a television interview on his return from the Azores, Pompidou said:

> There are Americans who say, who write and who think that the Common Agricultural Policy is harmful to the American economy and therefore the United States should try to make it more supple, that is to say, in the end make it disappear. Whether it is a matter of community preference, financial solidarity or unity of prices, these are established ideas in the defense of which the European farmer could count his obstinacy in defending their interests. In so doing we are defending the building of Europe. Everyone talks to us of integration and union, and yet in the only area where integration has been actually realized, they want to weaken it. At the moment the common agricultural market is weakened, at that moment there will be no hope for economic or monetary union, no further perspectives for political union.

COMPROMISE MEETINGS

The Azores meeting cleared the decks for the meeting of the finance ministers of Europe, Japan, Canada, and United States three days later which made the final compromise step toward realignment of the free world's currencies, including devaluation of the U.S. dollar at roughly 8 percent. This agreement was hailed by President Nixon as the "most significant monetary agreement in the history of the world."[3] Implied in the lower levels of the Washington bureaucracy but not stated by President Nixon was the Connally requirement that certain trade barriers would have to be removed before the United States could take the final step to seek approval of Congress for dollar devaluation. Out of this grew the third but much less dramatic diplomatic decision of December by the EC to sit down with the United States and begin formal discussion of long-standing complaints over European trade practices. A preliminary meeting was held in Brussels on December 21, 1971 leading to the formal opening of negotiations on January 14, 1972. The December meeting on trade problems coincided with the meeting of President Nixon and Prime Minister Edward Heath of Great Britain in Bermuda. Nixon took this occasion to bow to one of the major demands of the Common Market, Japan, and Canada: he announced removal of the 10 percent surcharge.

---

3. President Nixon on February 9, 1972, submitted the proposal to fix the value of gold at $38 U.S. dollars per ounce. This came after minor trade concessions had been made by the Common Market and Japan vs U.S. goods—chiefly oranges, tobacco, and chemicals.

REMOVAL OF SURCHARGE

Removal of the surcharge did much to lessen the tensions steadily rising between the United States and its European partners. It also calmed some of the fears of liberal trade advocates in the United States that the August announcement by the President had signaled a turn against the open trade policies of the past thirty-eight years. By now the United States had won some but not all of the demands set out in August.

The North Atlantic Treaty Organization (NATO) allies had voted to increase their contribution to European defense by $1 billion.

Removal of the surcharge had wide support in the United States, especially in the farm sector, though it admittedly weakened U.S. bargaining power in the formal trade negotiations ahead. Agricultural exports to the EC soared to $1.77 billion for the year ending June 30, 1971—up 25 percent from 1970 and a new record; U.S. farm interests did not want to endanger this trade. Europeans had hinted from time to time that American farm products could face new restrictions if the Common Market were pressed too strongly on other issues. However, the Community sidestepped direct retaliation and talked of special grants to industries and companies hurt by the import tax, which the United States also talked about. Removal of the surcharge reduced the possibility of these measures going into effect. However, the trade talks which began in January 1972 accomplished little more than a clarification of the positions of the various groups with some minor face-saving compromises on the agricultural issues.

DEMANDS BY AGRICULTURE

The principal demands of U.S. agriculture in the long-term trade negotiations are:

1. Easing of the Common Market's protectionist policy on agriculture.

2. Abandonment of the trade preference system widely used by the Common Market.

3. A call for an early round of negotiations in the General Agreement on Tariffs and Trade (GATT) to tackle nontariff barriers and other obstacles to freer trade.

The first of these demands has been before international bodies for years, with little if any effect. The United States is not entirely free of the charge of special protective devices for its agricultural products.

On the second issue, the United States in November 1971 made strong protests to the Common Market against the plan to allow special preferences to Austria, Sweden, Portugal, Finland, and Iceland—Euro-

pean Free Trade Association (EFTA) members left out of the new
alignment in the Community of Ten. The United States wanted such
preferential treatment postponed pending an international review. This
the Europeans called "madness" and went ahead preparing for the special preference arrangements for the EFTA members to take effect with
the full membership of Britain, Denmark, Norway, and Ireland in
January 1973. U.S. representatives to the Contracting Parties meeting
of GATT in Geneva on November 19 were rebuffed when they suggested that GATT go ahead and prepare new negotiations between the
enlarged Common Market and the other 80 GATT member countries.
Some delegates argued that this was not an urgent matter and could be
postponed. The Common Market delegates insisted that mid-1970s
would be the earliest date at which a new round of negotiations in
GATT could be considered.

It should be clear now to even the least observant that the days
during World War II and for nearly twenty years thereafter when the
United States with its sledgehammer of steel and gold could have its
way in international affairs are gone. The monetary realignment of
December 1971 was a negotiated deal, not dictated by the United States
as was the Bretton Woods Agreement of twenty years ago. The Commission of European Communities has flatly turned down the suggestion
that its preferential trade policy be halted. The U.S. request that the
European Community hold in storage at least 3 million bushels of
wheat rather than place it on a flooded market in third countries under
heavy subsidies of the Community provided for in the CAP was rejected.
However, the Community did agree to place 1.2 million tons in storage. Another *quid pro quo* for U.S. devaluation of the dollar included
items such as oranges—very sensitive politically in the United States,
where Florida and California interests argue that the CAP is costing
them $2.5 million annually. U.S. representatives argued that the 44
congressional votes from California and Florida might well make the
difference on whether Congress eventually approved the devaluation.[4]
The EC came right back with the argument that farm lobbies in Europe
are as powerful as they are in the United States, and "we have to face
elections too." They point out that the Common Market tariff structure
is lower than that of any major industrial nation and that U.S. exports
of agricultural products to the area have increased from $889 million
in 1958 to nearly $2 billion in 1970. The percentage increase of U.S.
exports going to the Market stands at 25 percent against an overall increase of 20 percent.

Periods of New Relations

The round of talks between the United States and the Community
early in 1972 clearly indicated that the United States was entering a new

---

4. The California and Florida representatives did go along with the dollar devaluation in the final House vote March 22, 1972.

period in relations with Europe. The new Community of Ten is flexing its muscles and with a degree of polite gusto telling the United States that "you are dealing with an equal now." President Pompidou closed his December 22, 1971, television interview with the assertion: "The United States has been forced to admit that Europe is an economic equal. . . . Washington now fears European economic power and competitiveness."

All of this points to tough bargaining bilaterally as well as through GATT in the years ahead. Some of the short-term issues are or will be compromised, but the really basic issues will be resolved only after long and hard bargaining among the three major trade powers of the free world—United States, the Common Market and Japan. Peter G. Peterson, Presidential Assistant for International Economic Affairs, in a report to the President in early 1972, warned:

The world has entered a period of great uncertainty in international economic affairs. Though the United States remains the largest single economic power, its postwar dominance of the non-Communist world is ended. . . . The institutions and rules governing internatinal trade and payments, created for a period of U.S. hegemony, must now be reconstructed to fit the reduced American role. The old system has become outgrown, outworn and increasingly crisis prone. The new period will be one of more flexible, enduring and visible economic relationships among nations.

The Peterson report merely emphasized what two presidents have tried to accomplish since the expiration in June 1967 of the Trade Expansion Act of 1962. While the chief executive of the United States from the beginning of the nation has had the power to "negotiate treaties of commerce and friendship" subject to the approval of Congress, the added powers for making or withholding concessions in international negotiations expired with the Act of 1962 (which was essentially an extension of the Reciprocal Trade Act). President Nixon in 1969 proposed, as had President Johnson before him, a new version of the Trade Expansion Act of 1962. Both versions gave the president greater power and flexibility in future negotiations and made more workable the provision for "assistance to industries damaged by the lower tariffs negotiated in previous sessions of GATT." Chairman Mills of the House Ways and Means Committee held hearings on President Nixon's proposed trade legislation during late 1969 and 1970. The measure passed the House in December 1970 and was before the Senate Foreign Relations Committee when the 91st Congress expired at the end of 1970. The measure—which had many restrictive and protective clauses in it designed mainly to pacify textile, shoe, ceramics, and chemical interests in the United States—was taken up again in 1971. An avalanche of protests from economists, trade groups, and agriculture forced abandonment of the bill. Mills, who had gone along with protection for the textile and shoe interests, withdrew his support of these provisions. The action in 1971 meant in practical terms that no trade policy

legislation would be passed until after the elections in 1978. In effect
the United States is operating under the old provisions of the Reciprocal
Trade Act of 1934, and the President during the interim has no power
to give or take away concessions in international negotiations, although
he does have power to negotiate treaties of friendship and commerce,
subject to the approval of the Congress.

Many observers of the international scene see the stage setting for
an international trade war in the decade ahead. Americans have been
slow to recognize this possibility, since only recently has the United
States had to bother much about trade expansion. Two major powers—
Japan and West Germany—rising from the ashes of World War II,
drew upon United States for capital, technology, food, and a host of
industrial items needed by much of the world to rebuild. Most nations
have now rebuilt, and their agricultural and industrial products are in
vigorous competition with U.S. products. There is increasing domestic
pressure in all of these countries to protect home industries. Where once
U.S. agricultural and industrial products were sought and welcomed—
including American investment capital—now doors are closing, and
almost every device known to ingenious bureaucrats is being introduced
to hold back the flood of products from various trading blocs and
groups. Only in Eastern Europe does there appear to be any move for
more open trade, and this is but a tiny crack in the wall which has sur-
rounded the Eastern bloc since World War II. Certainly the present
situation poses the necessity for the United States to search for alternatives in all sectors, with principal efforts in agriculture.

Some of the alternatives to be explored are:

1. A broader approach to international trade regulation (which is
now principally through GATT resolutions) which could include production control and regulation of agriculture and textiles and would
offer greater attention to the United Nations Conference on Trade and
Development in dealing with the problem of preferences.

2. Development of a free-trade area, beginning with U.S. and
Canadian elimination of customs and tariffs (but not a customs union).
Other willing nations could agree to the same reciprocal arrangements,
thus creating a major free-trade bloc. A study by a U.S.-Canadian committee, sponsored by the National Planning Association, concludes that
such an arrangement would materially increase efficiency in the industrial sectors of both countries, and, in the long term, Canadian income would increase by at least 10 percent.

3. Establishment of preferential trade areas; for example, give
special preference to Latin American products in the U.S. market.

4. An all-out drive to "establish international rules of competition,"
based on the experience of EFTA countries.

5. Gradual elimination of agricultural price supports, thus permitting agricultural prices to seek their own level in the world market.

(This is advocated by a major farm organization in the United States.)

6. Instant and severe retaliation under GATT rules when a product is unfairly discriminated against by any country.

7. Arming for an all-out trade war, meeting fire with fire, especially when American trade interests in third-country markets are threatened.

8. In the case of agriculture and other raw material products, an all-out drive for international agreements on prices and volume of trade.

Authority to use elements of each of the above alternates was present in some degree in the Trade Act of 1969 and was more explicit in the 1970 bill. None of these alternatives has been singled out as policy. It is generally admitted that in the light of mounting pressures in this country and the tendency of every country to want to protect its industry and the protectionist stance of the European Community and its new members, many paths to "freer" trade must be explored.

The United States, beginning with the New Deal in 1934, has pursued an inconsistent course in its trade policy. We used the reciprocal trade agreements to reduce barriers to international trade for two decades. Simultaneously, the Agricultural Adjustment Act of 1933 restricted farm imports and subsidized exports. Thus there have been efforts to expand international trade and also interference with trade demanded by farm programs. At a time when we were urging other countries against quantitative restrictions on imports, the Congress restricted imports. Under Section 22 of the Agricultural Adjustment Act, the United States has imposed import quotas on dairy products, and by so doing is clearly in violation of the GATT agreement. In any alternate policy, agriculture will be the rock around which much of the probing for new ways to "freer" trade will take place. In 1950 new legislation permitted actions to protect agriculture regardless of any trade or other international agreement.

During the hearings on the bill to extend the Trade Expansion Act of 1962, several groups pleaded vigorously for the cause of continued liberalized trade. One such group (called the Emergency Committee for American Trade and representing twenty-two of the largest industrial and trading firms in the United States) made a direct assault on protectionist proposals before the Congress, pointing out that the United States would be subject to quantitative limits "set not by competitive forces but by legislative fact."

The Emergency Committee warned that quotas would violate a fundamental policy of the U.S. government as well as the GATT. Committee spokesmen believed the countries affected would retaliate against U.S. products. It would be "retaliation to which we as the world's largest exporter are especially vulnerable."

In July 1967 David Rockefeller, an important member and leader of the Foreign Trade Association, appeared before the joint subcommittee on foreign economic policy and stated that the Kennedy Round, which had brought United States–Western Europe tariffs to an all-time low of about 8 percent, would be the last tariff-cutting session for some time. "The United States trade policy," he said, "will most likely face in the years ahead a completely different set of policy issues from those of the present." In his view, three issues merited special attention:

1. The problem of nontariff barriers.
2. The demand of many less-developed countries for some kind of preferential treatment.[5]
3. The pattern of U.S. trade relations with Canada, a particularly compelling issue in view of the steady expansion of regional trade arrangements in other parts of the world.

On the first point he concluded: "It would not make much sense to push further tariff reductions without first making some progress on prohibitive nontariff barriers." On the issue of preferences there was some alarm. Great Britain grants preferences to nations of the Commonwealth; the Common Market makes special preference arrangements with African countries. This means that United States, Latin America, and African nations outside the preference system are at a competitive disadvantage when exporting to European markets. While Rockefeller recognized the many obstacles to a U.S. preference system, he believed that such a system "might well exercise a powerful influence in expanding export earnings and promoting industrialization in less industrialized countries." On the final point of United States–Canadian trade relations he advised that it was essential for the United States to reconsider the feasibility of working toward free-trade arrangements.

George Ball, Under Secretary of State in the Kennedy administration, pointed his remarks before the subcommittee on American Republic affairs to the problem of United States–Latin American relations and the necessity for the Latin countries to achieve an adequate level of growth through their earnings. Ball ignored the United Nations Con-

5. Nathaniel Samuels in 1971 expressed deep concern at the growing extension of the preference system throughout Europe: "The creation of an even wider preference area cannot be the objective of American policy. If this proves to be the road ahead, then we will have to rethink our entire position."
On July 22, 1972, Sweden, Austria, Iceland, Portugal, Switzerland, and tiny Liechtenstein signed treaties with the Common Market Six setting up preferential arrangements for formal associate membership with the Market to become effective in first stages on the formal establishment of the Community of Ten January 1, 1973. Finland will be added later. Each nation pledges itself to begin immediately to reduce its tariffs and trade restrictions with a total free-trade area to be established by July 1, 1977. This will create a free-trade area of 16 European nations, with a population of 300 million, the largest single trade bloc in the world and the most highly industrialized area in the world. This represents a major defeat for U.S. policy, as noted above, which has been to stall the preferential treatment of countries outside the Common Market until an international conference could be held and guidelines for such action established by international negotiation.

ference on Trade and Development arguments in favor of a general preference system by the industrialized nations to all of the developing countries. However, he did concede that with trading blocs growing more protectionist in their behavior and with more difficulty in negotiating meaningful liberalization of trade, there would be large support in Latin America should the United States set up a special trading system for the hemisphere in which Latins would receive favorable treatment, much as Puerto Rico does today.

Thus is drawn the issue of an "open system" which the United States has consistently urged during the last thirty-seven years or a "closed system" which is characterized by the Eastern European bloc and increasingly by the Western European bloc.

The Nixon administration has promised Latin American countries expanded trade opportunities in the American market. In a comprehensive policy statement before the General Assembly of the Organization of American States at San José, Costa Rica, in April 1971, Secretary of State William P. Rogers declared: "The administration will make a concerted effort to win early congressional approval for trade preferences sought by Latin American states." He promised efforts to abolish all tariffs on some 500 items, mostly manufactured and semi-manufactured goods. The 500 items mentioned represent $650 million worth of trade presently under a tariff average of 8 percent.

The storm which the Trade Act of 1970 generated at home and abroad is but further evidence that the problem will not be settled for a long time. Will the semiopen system symbolized by GATT and other multilateral efforts of the United Nations continue and prevail? Or will the creeping preference system in the Common Market and the continued formation of regional trading blocs force the United States into some sort of a free-trade or preference system arrangement? In all these efforts at trade liberalization and protection of particular segments of some economies, agriculture will loom as a central problem.

While general trade legislation is in somewhat of a stall with little prospect of real progress until 1973 or later, signs point to a general shift away from the 25-year-old refusal of United States to restore normal trade relations with the Soviet Union and the Eastern European bloc. Late in 1971 Maurice Stans, then Secretary of Commerce, visited Russia and opened prolonged discussions on liberalization of trade between the two countries—among other things the extension of credits to Russia for the purchase of industrial goods. Stans saw a possible $2 billion trade developing in this sector. In mid-1972 Earl Butz, Secretary of Agriculture, visited Russia along with Assistant Secretary of Agriculture for International Relations, Clarence D. Palmby, and negotiated a major sale of feed grains.[6] Prior to President Nixon's visit to the People's

---

6. In mid-1972 President Nixon announced an agreement with Russia on $750 million worth of wheat and feed grains on most-favored-nation terms, to be completed over a three-year period. Terms of the sale will require congressional approval.

Republic of China in early 1972 some of the restrictions on U.S. trade with that country were lifted.

Many of the administration experts and some of the politicians up for election in 1972 were relieved that they did not have to face the issue of freer vs more restricted trade that major trade legislation would be bound to present. It appears that no effort will be made to take up any trade liberalization or a new trade act before 1973.

The legislation which finally wins approval of the Congress will undoubtedly be influenced by the talks and negotiations going on with our own partners of the free world as well as the broadening and more cordial relations with the Communist nations. In the meantime, so far as special powers of the executive department to influence trade are concerned, the United States has been operating under a do-nothing trade policy since June 30, 1967, when the Trade Expansion Act of 1962 expired. However, world trade goes on. Importers are importing and exporters are exporting. Even with the doleful rhetoric in some quarters, U.S. farm exports to the Common Market rose in 1970 by 20 percent though the CAP still remains the symbol of evil. This probably adds up to the fact that the status quo, in trade as well as in business, is sometimes fairly satisfactory.

GLOSSARY

BOUND PRODUCTS are products admitted to the Common Market duty-free under terms of previous tariff negotiations of GATT. Soybeans and cotton are U.S. examples of such products.

COMMON AGRICULTURAL POLICY (CAP) refers broadly to EC's overall policy of changing from an individual country's agricultural program to an essentially uniform system of production and marketing through the area with free interstate trade for nearly all agricultural commodities and a common external tariff and regulations for trade outside the area. Central to the CAP is a single system of regulated prices.

COMMON MARKET is the general term used to describe the grouping of six West European States—Luxembourg, Belgium, the Netherlands, France, the Federal Republic of West Germany, and Italy—under the Treaty of Rome in 1958 creating a custom's union and providing for the economic integration of these countries. The original official designation, the European Economic Community, has been contracted to the European Community as the official name. Other terms used to describe the Market in this book are the Community, Inner Six, the Six, EC, EEC, and European Common Market.

CONTRACTING PARTIES refers to the grouping of governments which have fully acceded to GATT acting collectively. The work of GATT is administered by a secretariat under a Director General. The Contracting Parties meet at least once each year in general session to discuss developments in international trade and to develop work programs which are delegated to a Council of members. Active committee work goes on between sessions.

173

COUNCIL FOR MUTUAL COOPERATION (Comecon) is a grouping of nations in the Soviet bloc designed originally as an economic backup for member states of the Warsaw Pact Organization. The original members of the treaty organization are Albania, Bulgaria, Czechoslovakia, Hungary, Poland, Romania, the Soviet Zone of Germany (East Germany), and the Soviet Union. Members at various times have broken away from the common defense arrangements provided in the twenty-year treaty. Albania, for example, has increasingly aligned itself with Communist China. Romania has not always cooperated fully in the organization.

COUNCIL FOR MUTUAL ECONOMIC ASSISTANCE (CMEA) is synonymous with Comecon. It involves the same state signatories as the Warsaw Pact. However, the stress is on interstate trade and economic development. In more recent years it has moved toward providing machinery for international trade between the Communist countries and other parts of the world through an international banking system.

COUNTERVAILING DUTIES are used mainly by the United States as instruments of protection for agricultural and a few other products. They are essentially a protective surtax to offset a subsidy or export payment by an exporting country. When assessed, countervailing duties are in addition to other duties normally paid.

ECONOMIC COMMISSION FOR EUROPE (ECE) is composed of Western and Eastern European states and functions mainly as a forum for discussion of trade matters between Eastern Europe and Western countries. It also keeps trade statistics and other information relative to the two major trading areas. The organization grew out of the Geneva conference to promote East-West trade in 1950. This is a formal regional economic organization outside the U.N. dealing with economic matters in both Eastern and Western Europe to which the United States belongs.

EUROPEAN COAL AND STEEL COMMUNITY (ECSC) is a grouping of six European nations set up May 1, 1953, to establish a free market for steel and coal within the Community. Original members: France, Italy, West Germany, the Netherlands, Belgium, Luxembourg.

EUROPEAN FREE TRADE ASSOCIATION (EFTA), sometimes referred to as the Outer Seven, is a regional grouping of seven West European states set up by the Stockholm Convention in 1960 and completed in December 1960. The states involved in this grouping are the United Kingdom, Norway, Denmark, Sweden, Switzerland, Austria, and Portugal, with Finland as an associate member. It is essentially a free-trade area between the member states. Interstate tariffs and quotas were completely abolished by the end of 1966 on manufactured goods. Agriculture, except industrial products derived from farm production, was never included in the arrangement. There is no common external tariff as in the case of the Common Market, each member making its own external trade arrangements. There is regulation on the disposition of imported goods within the area.

FIXED TARIFF refers to a list or schedule of articles of merchandise with the rate of duty to be paid to the government for their importation. Such tariffs are usually fixed by international negotiations and subject to change only by the executive branch of the government involved and, so far as tariffs arrived at in international negotiations, subject to the rules of the General Agreement on Tariffs and Trade.

GATE PRICE is the minimum import price used by the EC in connection with its Common Agricultural Policy on poultry, eggs, and pork. Theoretically it is based on representative costs of production in non-EC exporting countries. The same for all EC countries with respect to commodities covered, it is fixed in advance for a three-month period.

GENERAL AGREEMENT ON TARIFFS AND TRADE (GATT) is a multilateral agreement negotiated in 1947 among 23 countries including the United States to increase international trade by reducing tariffs and other trade barriers. As of 1971, 66 countries have full participant status, 7 belong under special arrangements, 6 participate provisionally. The GATT countries account for 85 percent of all world trade. Six general tariff conferences have been held under this agreement: Geneva, Switzerland, 1947; Annecy, France, 1949; Torquay, England, 1950–51; Geneva, 1956; Geneva, 1960–61 (sometimes referred to as the "Dillon Round" for C. Douglas Dillon, Secretary of the Treasury under President Dwight Eisenhower); Geneva, 1964–67 (called the "Kennedy Round"). It was in the Kennedy Round that for the first time the six states of the Common Market negotiated as one party. This has major implications for the future of GATT when the Common Market is enlarged to ten or more member states with a common external tariff.

INTERVENTION means an action taken by the EC, usually purchases of products offered, to assure Common Market farmers that price objectives of the CAP will be met.

INTERVENTION LEVIES are higher levies which are applied against imported goods when prices within the Common Market for that particular item have dropped below the support levels set by the Common Market authority.

INTERVENTION PRICES, comparable to the U.S. support price system, is the price applicable to certain commodities at which the EC makes direct purchases to provide price protection to its farmers.

KENNEDY ROUND was the sixth negotiating session of the members of GATT meeting in Geneva from 1964 to 1967 and was named for the late President John F. Kennedy, under whose leadership the Trade Expansion Act of 1962 was passed by the U.S. Congress. This act set the stage for U.S. participation in the negotiation sessions which were later hailed by some as the most comprehensive ever held.

NORTH ATLANTIC TREATY ORGANIZATION (NATO) is a treaty signed in Washington, D.C., August 24, 1949, by Belgium, Canada, Denmark, France, Iceland, Italy, Luxembourg, the Netherlands, Norway, Portugal, the United Kingdom, and the United States. Greece, Turkey, and West Germany joined later.

ORGANIZATION FOR ECONOMIC COOPERATION AND DEVELOPMENT (OECD), a trade group set up in 1961 by 18 member nations plus the OEEC, the United States, and Canada to coordinate Western nations' economic aid programs and link the six nations of the Common Market and the seven European Free Trade Association countries into a common plan mainly for extending aid to developing countries, provides a forum for international trade policy discussions.

ORGANIZATION FOR EUROPEAN ECONOMIC COOPERATION (OEEC), a group of nations participating in the Marshall Plan, serves in general coordination, planning, and information for the participating nations.

RECIPROCAL TRADE AGREEMENTS refer to a system of reciprocity whereby a concession in trade arrangements with a given nation is offset by an equal concession to the other nation. With the Reciprocal Trade Agreement Act in 1934 the United States offered and gave equal concessions under the most-favored-nation clause to all other countries making similar concessions. After the creation of GATT in 1947, the most-favored-nation treatment was usually afforded all GATT signatories. However, there have been some exceptions to this general rule with some of the Eastern European countries.

SUPPLEMENTARY LEVY is an additional amount, subject to change at any time, assessed on imports when the EC determines that the product is being offered by outside countries at less than the gate price.

TARGET PRICE (GUIDE PRICE) is the level which the European Community wants wholesale market prices to approximate under the CAP. In some instances there is a producer target price as well as a market target. Olive oil is one example.

THIRD-COUNTRY MARKETS are those areas outside the formal trading blocs of EC, EFTA, and the United States in which products come in direct competition for markets.

UNITED NATIONS CONFERENCE ON TRADE AND DEVELOPMENT (UNCTAD) grew out of a meeting held in Switzerland in 1964 called by the member states of the United Nations Economic and Social Council. The purpose of the meeting was an attempt by less-developed nations to change the structure of international trade to better meet the needs of the developing nations. It was attended by 2,000 delegates from 119 countries. Two major recommendations were made with respect to agriculture: (1) guidelines for international community agreements; (2) an action program to reduce tariff and nontariff barriers on products, mostly agricultural, of developing countries. Continuing machinery was established. Conferences are held every three years. The permanent executive body is a Trade Development Board composed of 55 members, which meets twice yearly.

VARIABLE LEVIES are charges on imports designed to keep the import price above that of the domestic product. They are automatically increased or decreased to effect changes in import prices.

BIBLIOGRAPHY

BOOKS

Butterwick, Michael, and Rolfe, Edmund Neville. *Food, Farming and the Common Market*. Oxford University Press, New York and Toronto, 1968.

Coppock, John O. *North Atlantic Policy, the Agricultural Gap.* Twentieth Century Fund Study, 1963.

Geiger, Theodore. *Transatlantic Relations in Prospect of an Enlarged European Community*. National Planning Association, 1970.

Kraft, Joseph. *The Grand Design*. Harper Brothers, 1962.

BULLETINS, REPORTS, AND SURVEYS

Andrews, Stanley. *A Review and Appraisal of Agricultural Production, Structure and International Agricultural Trade in Six Countries of Eastern Europe*. Andreas Foundation, 1967.

Andrews, Stanley. *The Common Market: Its Implications for American Agriculture*. Andreas Foundation, 1968.

Basic Statistics of the Community. Statistical Office of the European Communities, 1967.

Building European Free Trade Association. EFTA Secretariat, Geneva, 1966.

Common Market Farm Front. Official version of Council of Ministers' actions issued by Washington office of the European Communities.

Common Market's External Trade, 1958–1967. European Communities Information Office, Mar. 1969.

Economic Commission for Europe. *Annual Review of Trade and Economic Development*. Geneva, Switzerland, 1966.

177

Economic Research Service, USDA. *The Agricultural Situation in Communist Areas.* Annual reviews, 1966–1971.

Economic Research Service, USDA. *European Community's Common Agricultural Policy,* Oct. 1969.

Economic Research Service, USDA. *European Free Trade Association Agricultural Trade Statistics, 1961–1967.* Foreign No. 271, June 1969.

European Community. *The Facts.* Brussels, Belgium, 1971.

European Free Trade Association. Ninth Annual Report. Geneva, Switzerland, 1969.

Food and Agriculture Organization of the United Nations. *State of Food and Agriculture.* Annual reports, 1958–1971.

Foreign Agricultural Service, USDA. Annual estimates of world trade in agricultural products, 1960–1971.

Future United States Trade Policy. Report to the President by Special Representative for Trade Negotiations, Jan. 1969.

National Planning Association Reports: The European Common Market and American Agriculture, Vol. 2, Sept. 1963; International Questions Facing Britain, the United States, and Canada, Vol. 19, Mar. 1971; A World of Trading Blocs, Vol. 19, Apr. 1971; A Turning Point in World Trade Policy—An American View, Vol. 19, June 1971.

Schmidt, H., and Grunewald, L. Institut fur Wirtschaftsforschung, Aggregation of Future Demand and Supply for Agricultural Products in the European Community, 1970–75. Munich, Germany, 1969.

Periodicals

Christian Science Monitor. Dispatches on actions of the Commission and Council of Ministers.

Cleveland, Harold V. The Common Market after DeGaulle. *Foreign Affairs Quarterly,* July 1969.

The Reporter. Monthly review issued by Washington office of EFTA.

Peterson, Peter G. America Still Top Producer but . . . *US News and World Report,* July 12, 1971.

INDEX

Adenauer, Konrad, 5
Adjustment assistance, 155
African products, 81, 87–89
Agricultural Adjustment Act, 117, 169
Agriculture
  changes in Eastern Europe, 91–100
  Communist control, 91–98
  future implications, 148–51
  under GATT, 120–21
  importance in Common Market, 9–11,
    124–25
  and Treaty of Rome, 12–17
  U.S. and Common Market, 29–33, 118–
    20, 157, 159
  U.S. demands in GATT, 165
Albania, 40
Algeria, 86
Annual Review of Trade, 38
Argentina, 67, 120
Arshua Convention, 89
Associate states, 72, 79, 81, 85–90
  full association, 85
  limited association, 85–86
  special association, 88–90
Association Convention, 79
Atlantic Community, 10, 55, 62, 91. *See
  also* Grand Design; Political integra-
  tion; United States of Europe
  background, 55–57
  failure, 58–60
Australia, 134

Austria, 34, 35, 38, 49, 72, 77, 86, 90, 105,
  114, 129, 136, 150, 165

Ball, George, 170
Belgium, 4, 6, 21, 32, 34, 69, 70, 83, 84,
  87, 125, 146
Bilateral trade, 72–73, 107–8, 114, 125,
  148, 160, 167
Brazil, 87
Briand, Aristide, 4
Brodie, Henry, 121
Brown, George, 41, 48
Bulgaria, 9, 40, 91, 94, 96–98, 101–8, 136
Butter surplus, 33, 77. *See also* Soybean
  products
Butz, Earl, 171

Canada, 34, 59, 67, 90, 120, 131, 150, 157,
  162, 164, 168, 170
  trade relations with U.S., 170
Castro, Fidel, 55
"Chicken war," 30, 78, 114, 156
China, 116, 117, 151, 172
Churchill, Winston, 4
Collectivization, 93
Common Agricultural Policy (CAP), 18–
  24, 31–32, 49, 52, 60, 62, 68, 70, 73–74,
  123–24, 127, 136, 138–39, 141, 148,
  151, 164, 166, 172
  basic agreements, 17
  basic assumptions, 22–23

179

DATE DUE

DISPLAY			
MAY 1 0 1983			
MAY 1 0 1983			
MAR 5 '85			
FEB 2 5 '85			
MAY 1 9 '87			
MAY 1 3 '87			
DEC 1 8 1996			
GAYLORD			PRINTED IN U.S.A.